How To
WIN The
WINE
GAME

PETER NOBLE &
PENNY LANDEAU

VERMILION

LONDON

ACKNOWLEDGMENTS

Such a wide ranging topic has required help and advice from many trade experts all over the world and we are so grateful to everyone who has so freely given their time and expertise. In particular we want to thank Colin Gurteen, our technical editor – former Controller of Studies, Wine & Spirit Education Trust; Rosemary George MW, who contributed to the tasting comments in the shelf guide; Dr. Peter Hallgarten the authority on the Rhône and Germany; Roger Voss who contributed technical information for the guides; Geoff Taylor, wine chemist of Corkwise Ltd who provided the data for the acidity and tannin chart; David Wolfe gave us invaluable help with the food and wine sector. Encouragement and constructive help came from Liz Robertson MW, John Davy, and Patricia Monahan. Jeremy Bullmore was the inspiration for the title. Judith Hamp originated the design for the illustration on pp.10–11.

From abroad: our warm thanks to the authorities in New Zealand, Hungary, Bulgaria and Australia, to our friends Johnny Hugel in Alsace, Bob Mondavi and Warren Winiarski in California and Ted Hughes in South Africa.

Back at base, Julia Trustram-Eve did invaluable early research, Bonni Emms has been our Project Co-ordinator and worked throughout with us on the format, Kay Hillier deserves a medal for typing and retyping the text with such good humour and Sue Akester, Clive and Lucy Stapley and the late Pat Bell have given much constructive comment.

Published in 1993 by Vermilion
an imprint of Ebury Press
Random House
20 Vauxhall Bridge Road
London SW1V 2SA

Text © Peter Noble & Penny Landeau 1993

A catalogue record for this book is available from the British Library.

ISBN 0 09 177022 X

Designed and typeset by Blackjacks, London

Cover illustration by Tony Hanniford
Playing the Game cartoon by Mathew Lawrence for The Grape Connection
All other illustrations and washes by Ian Sidaway

Printed in Italy by New Interlitho S.p.A. - Milan

How To
Win The
Wine
Game

CONTENTS

INTRODUCTION

WHITE WINE GUIDES

RED WINE GUIDES

THE AUTHORS

Peter Noble CBE is one of the UK's leading wine experts. His enthusiasm for the subject is infectious and his desire to share his delight is positively missionary. Formerly was Managing Director of Christopher & Co., wine merchants

to HM The Queen and Chairman of the Wine Development Board and the Wine & Spirit Association, Peter is currently President of the EC Wine & Importers' Group and co-founder of The Grape Connection.

Penny Landeau has a background in business and arts administration. She set up The Grape Connection with Peter in 1987 to develop his concept into practical systems and products which would make wine more accessible. With her firmly consumer-orientated attitude, Penny has questioned and challenged the traditional methods of the wine trade to produce a refreshingly simple solution to the problems of choosing wine.

A NEW APPROACH TO WINE

Why should it be so difficult to discover which wines we like? Why are the labels so confusing? Why do some labels give information in one way and others use a completely different system?

Thirty years ago, nearly all our wine came from just five regions of France, so choosing a bottle of wine was comparatively simple. Today, there are around 20,000 labels from 35 countries and countless regions. No wonder the average buyer is confused and even the knowledgeable stick to familiar names.

We decided it was time to shed some light on the arcane world of wine. We were convinced it was possible to produce a system which would allow anyone to understand wine and, more importantly, find the wines they like. During four years of research we have tested our system on over 5,000 people at our public events – and it works!

How To Win The Wine Game is the culmination of our endeavours. It encapsulates a DIY system for identifying the wines YOU like and it is simple.

There are just 11 classic grapes, five red and six white, which make up 80% of the Quality wine on the shelves. Each grape variety has very distinctive flavours and characteristics, so first you need to know which varieties suit you. Then you can decide which style you prefer and learn which regions produce that style. To select the right bottle you finally need to know how it will be labelled because the name of the grape does not appear on half the bottles. GRAPE, STYLE, LABEL. This, in a nutshell, is the core of our system.

We have tried to blow away the mystique and snobbery surrounding wine and hope that these guides will lead you to the wines you enjoy. After all, at the end of the day, it is *your* taste, and no one else's, that matters. **How to Win the Wine Game** does not set out to make you a Master of Wine – simply a master of your own taste.

Peter Noble & Penny Landeau.

**PLEASE READ THE FOLLOWING SECTION before
using the guides, since it explains THE SYSTEM and
PLAYING THE GAME.
The guides may then be used in any order.**

THE GUIDES

How to Win the Wine Game
is divided into individual guides
which feature the 11 classic grapes
and the traditional and world
famous wine regions where they
are grown – France (Bordeaux,
Burgundy and the Rhône) and
Germany.

Each guide comprises:
• THE SYSTEM •

KNOW YOUR GRAPE

a general introduction to each grape variety

KNOW YOUR STYLE

introducing the **STYLOMETER**, an at-a-glance guide to the styles of wine
produced in each region

MAKE THE GRAPE CONNECTION

shows you how to find the wines you like, with a guide to the grape
names and their synonyms, behind the regional labels

• APPLYING THE SYSTEM •
PLAYING THE GAME

a game of wine man's bluff – but the bottles are masked, not the players! We suggest some wines which will give interesting comparisons, or you can make your own selection from the WHAT'S ON THE SHELVES sections

• BUYING THE WINE •
WHAT'S ON THE SHELVES

clearly laid out by region, taste, vintage and price

RELIABLE PRODUCERS & SHIPPERS
some of the names to look for on the labels

(**NB** These guides focus on still, unfortified wine. Fortified and sparkling wines and indigenous grape varieties will be the subject of future guides.)

The following symbols are used for easy reference throughout this book.

A–D   **Price bands** **A** up to £5.00   **B** £5.00 to £7.50
                            C £7.50 to £10.00 **D** over £10.00

 Good years though not necessarily ready for drinking

 Where no good years are shown (Eastern Europe) there is little choice so take whatever is readily available

 When to drink – buy Southern Hemisphere wines one year younger than Northern Hemisphere due to the different harvest times

THE SYSTEM

• KNOW YOUR GRAPE •
• KNOW YOUR STYLE •
• MAKE THE GRAPE CONNECTION •

Our system is based firstly on the premise that personal taste is dictated by the grape variety and then by the style of the wine. Secondly, that choosing wine is far more difficult than it need be, due to the conflicting labelling system.

KNOW YOUR GRAPE

The GRAPE produces the FLAVOUR.
There are many different varieties of grape, each with its own distinctive flavours so it is vital to know which grapes suit you.

KNOW YOUR STYLE

**STYLE comes mainly from the CLIMATE
and the WINEMAKER (see p.200)**
The word 'Style' is used to encompass all the factors other than the grape variety that contribute to the taste, aroma and colour of wine (e.g. whether it is light or full, dry or sweet, how it is made, etc).

MAKE THE GRAPE CONNECTION

Much of Western Europe still labels traditionally by region, with no mention of the grape on the label, whilst the rest of the world labels by the grape variety. So, once you know which grapes and style you prefer, in each guide you will find the varietal names behind the regional labels.

KNOW YOUR GRAPE

The taste of wine is primarily dictated by the grape variety. Four out of every five bottles of Quality wine on the shelves are made from just 11 classic* grape varieties

CHARDONNAY
The great white grape of Burgundy, now grown successfully in most of the world's major wine regions. It varies from light to full-bodied, from the crisp green apple flavour of Chablis to full, fruity mouthfuls from parts of Australia and California.

RIESLING
Perhaps the world's most aristocratic white grape, Riesling is at its best in Germany but is grown in many countries. Its reputation has suffered from cheap and often unpleasant 'look-alikes'. The wines range from very dry to very sweet, never too cloying because of the high acidity. The flavour is aromatic, becoming rich and honeyed as the wines get sweeter.

GEWURZTRAMINER
Gewürztraminer makes pungent, perfumed wines, usually on the dry side and easy to recognise. They are spicy, with a smell of lychees, low in acidity and quite high in alcohol.

CHENIN BLANC
The most widely planted grape of the Loire, producing wines from searingly dry to luscious and sweet. High acidity makes them refreshing when dry and prevents them from being cloying when sweet. They have flowery flavours that become honeyed as they age.

SAUVIGNON BLANC
This is the classic white grape of the Loire (Sancerre and Pouilly Fumé), now grown world-wide, producing dry, aromatic wines with a pungent smell, high acidity and a pronounced green goose-berry flavour. It is widely used in Bordeaux both as a single variety and for blending with the Sémillon grape

SEMILLON
The major white grape of Bordeaux, where it produces – often with Sauvignon Blanc – both dry and very sweet wines. It is one of

* Classic grapes produce the world's finest wines and are widely grown and distributed around the world

Australia's premier grapes but there the wines have been traditionally dry. Now, fine sweet wines are made to compete with the best from Bordeaux. The flavour of Sémillon changes from lemony when young, to a rich, honeyed taste when mature.

CABERNET SAUVIGNON
Currently the most popular red variety grown worldwide. The wines have a pronounced smell and taste of blackcurrants, often with extra flavours of mint, herbs and cedar. They are high in tannin so age well but take time to mature. In Bordeaux, Cabernet Sauvignon is the more famous of the two major red grapes, the other being Merlot, with which it is invariably blended.

MERLOT
Merlot is one of the two major red grapes in Bordeaux, where it is blended with Cabernet Sauvignon. As a single variety, Merlot is now gaining popularity elsewhere in both France and the major wine-growing countries. The wines are lower in tannin and acidity than those made with Cabernet Sauvignon, so are easier to drink when young. They are soft and smooth, with plum and fruitcake flavours.

PINOT NOIR
This is the great red grape of Burgundy, where it is generally accepted as being at its best. Although grown in many countries, it is capricious by nature, and outside France seldom achieves the style or taste of Burgundy. The wines are soft and perfumed, usually pale in colour with complex flavours and a hint of sweetness.

SYRAH
The only red grape of the Northern Rhône, Syrah is commonly used for blending in the Southern Rhône and throughout the south of France and is known as Shiraz in Australia. It produces dense, purple-coloured wines with rich, often spicy fruit flavours, and is usually very tannic when young.

GRENACHE
Grenache, the most important red grape of the Southern Rhône, is also widely used in the south of France and in Spain where, as Garnacha, it is important in Rioja wines. Pale in colour but high in alcohol, the wines have a herbal, sometimes peppery flavour.

NB: The GAMAY grape is not included here as it is not a classic variety. It is included in BEHIND THE RED BURGUNDY LABEL *(p.109)* as it accounts for a large percentage of red wine produced in Burgundy, including Beaujolais.

KNOW YOUR STYLE

Once you know the grapes that suit you, there are still hundreds of bottles to choose from, so you need to know which *style* you prefer. What does style denote? *(see p.200)*. Most people, quite rightly, take style to mean either light, medium and full **or** dry, medium and sweet, but there are other factors such as tannin and oak-ageing *(see p.204)* which contribute to it. A good wine is said to be well balanced when all the main ingredients – fruit, acidity, tannin and alcohol – are in the right proportions *(see p.202)*. To help you select the right bottles from the hundreds confronting you, we have devised our STYLOMETER. This covers both dry to sweet (whites only) and light to full (red and whites) as appropriate.

DRY   MEDIUM   SWEET

(white wines only)

Four classic white grapes, Riesling, Gewürztraminer, Chenin Blanc and Semillon, produce wines which cover the spectrum from dry to sweet either naturally or with the winemakers intervention.

STYLOMETER

DRY

ITALY	Trentino Alto-Adige	
NEW ZEALAND	South Island	Canterbury, Otago, Marlborough
FRANCE	Alsace	
GERMANY	Rhein	Pfalz, Baden (Kabinett wines)
AUSTRIA	Burgenland, Styria	
USA	Oregon	
FRANCE	Alsace	(Grand Cru and most 'Vendange Tardive' wines)

MEDIUM

AUSTRIA	Burgenland, Styria	(Spätlese wines)
GERMANY	Rhein	Pfalz, Baden (Spätlese wines)
CROATIA	Kutjevo	
SLOVENIA	Lutomer	
NEW ZEALAND	North Island	Gisborne
AUSTRALIA	South Australia	
USA	California	Mendocino, Napa Valley, Sonoma County
SOUTH AFRICA	Paarl, Stellenbosch	
FRANCE	Alsace	('Vendange Tardive' wines in exceptional years)

SWEET

NEW ZEALAND	North Island	(Late Harvest)
GERMANY	Rhein	Pfalz, Baden (Beerenauslese and Trockenbeerenauslese)
AUSTRIA	Burgenland, Styria	(Beerenauslese and Trockenbeerenauslese)
FRANCE	Alsace	(Sélection de grains nobles – rare)
SOUTH AFRICA	Paarl, Stellenbosch	(Late Harvest)
USA	California	(Late Harvest)

LIGHT   MEDIUM   FULL

LIGHT   MEDIUM   FULL

(red and white wines)

This is the 'weight' or 'body' of a wine, i.e. the combination of alcohol, fruit and acids, and is largely determined by region/climate. In general, the lighter styles come from cooler climates because the grapes are seldom as ripe as in warmer climates.

STYLOMETER

As Cabernet Sauvignon is a late-ripening variety, warm climates produce the ripest fruit and thus, easy-to-drink wines.

LIGHT

NEW ZEALAND	South Island	Marlborough
ITALY	Trentino Alto-Adige	
	Friuli-Venezia-Giulia	
AUSTRALIA	Tasmania	
	Victoria	Yarra Valley
FRANCE	Côteaux d'Aix en Provence	
	Côtes de Provence	
	Languedoc-Roussillon	Vins de Pays D'Oc
NEW ZEALAND	North Island	Gisborne, Hawkes Bay, Henderson

MEDIUM

ITALY	Veneto	
AUSTRALIA	Victoria	Yarra Valley
	South Australia	Coonawarra
	Western Australia	Margaret River, Mt Barker
CROATIA	Istria	
SLOVENIA		
ITALY	Umbria, Emilia Romagna	
AUSTRALIA	Southern Australia	Clare, Adelaide Hill, McLaren Vale
USA	Washington	Yakima Valley, Columbia River Basin
ROMANIA	Murfatlar	
USA	California	Monterey
BULGARIA	Plovdiv	
USA	California	Central Napa, Central Sonoma

FULL

BULGARIA	Sukindol, Svishtov, Russe	
CHILE	Maipo, Curico	
SPAIN	Penedés	
SOUTH AFRICA	most regions	
ITALY	Tuscany	
AUSTRALIA	New South Wales	Hunter Valley, Riverina
	South Australia	Barossa Valley
	Western Australia	Swan Valley
USA	California	Northern Napa Valley, Riverside

MAKE THE GRAPE CONNECTION

The purpose of **How To Win the Wine Game** is to make wine selection easier. Once you have decided on which grapes and style you prefer, you have to beat the problem of finding your way through a conflicting labelling system. Much of western Europe traditionally label by region, with no mention of the grape variety. On the other hand, the rest of the world does label by the grape variety. Therefore each guide shows the grape varietal names and their synonyms behind the regional labels.

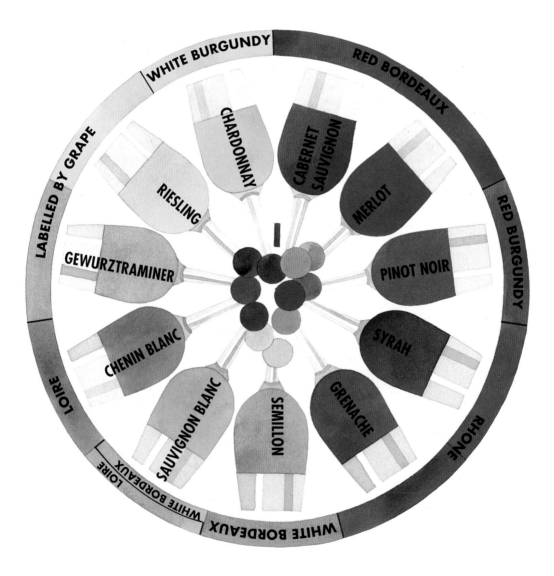

...AND MASTER THE TWO WAYS OF LABELLING WINE

It is vital to know the link between the two ways of labelling wine,
as both appear on the shelves.

BOTH WINES BELOW ARE MADE 100% FROM THE CHARDONNAY GRAPE

LABELLED BY REGION

RÉCOLTE DU DOMAINE
CHABLIS GRAND CRU
VAUDÉSIR
APPELLATION CONTROLÉE
MIS EN BOUTEILLE PAR
JOSEPH DROUHIN
Maison fondée en 1880
NÉGOCIANT A BEAUNE, COTE-D'OR
AUX CELLIERS DES ROIS DE FRANCE ET DES DUCS DE BOURGOGNE
13 % vol.   FRANCE   75 cl

LABELLED BY GRAPE

EMBOTELLADO EN LA PROPIEDAD
JEAN LEON
1988

Chardonnay
«PENEDES»
DENOMINACION DE ORIGEN
TORRELAVID · ESPAÑA
75 cl.   13.5% Vol.
Bot Nº   *Jean Leon*
Jean Leon, S.A

BOTH WINES BELOW ARE MADE 100% FROM THE PINOT NOIR GRAPE

LABELLED BY REGION

BOURGOGNE
APPELLATION BOURGOGNE CONTROLÉE

MIS EN BOUTEILLE PAR JOSEPH DROUHIN
CÔTE-D'OR · 21200 FRANCE
AUX CELLIERS DES ROIS DE FRANCE ET
DES DUCS DE BOURGOGNE
12,5 % vol.   FRANCE   75 cl

LABELLED BY GRAPE

1990
Napa Valley
PINOT NOIR
ALCOHOL 13% BY VOLUME
PRODUCED AND BOTTLED BY
ROBERT MONDAVI WINERY
OAKVILLE, CALIFORNIA

PLAYING THE GAME

There is no substitute for practical experience. The best way to learn which grapes, countries and regions match your taste is to compare one wine against another. PLAYING THE GAME comes after the system in each guide and we suggest wines which will provide an interesting comparison when entertaining friends or family. We find it an enjoyable way to discover our own, as well as others' tastes.

MASKING THE LABELS

Tasting wine requires no mystique or ceremony, just good company and some masking labels. Why mask the labels? Well, who has not been swayed by a glossy or sophisticated label only to be disappointed by the wine? Even the experts are biased by the label. If the wines are similarly priced, the better known or familiar will often influence your judgment. Where there are two bottles of differing price, most people expect the more expensive to be better. So, mask the labels. You will then taste without prejudice and in turn explode a few myths.

We have designed our own colourful and reusable masking labels – see ORDER FORM (p.224) or simply cover the bottles in your own way.

PREPARING YOUR WINES FOR TASTING

- Remove any lead or plastic cap from the top of the bottle which will give away the grower's or shipper's name.

- Scrape off any neck label, as this too identifies the wine.

- Place the masking labels around the bottles. If possible, get someone who is not tasting to do this for you. If you do it yourself, turn the labels away from you and muddle the bottles up before attaching the masking labels.

- When tasting over a meal, fill the glasses up to a third full. This leaves room for the wine to be swirled around in the glass, which releases the all-important aroma.

- If you are entertaining large numbers, you should get 16 good tasting samples per bottle. It is useful to have an empty bottle and funnel for any unwanted wine.

HOW TO TASTE

Here are some basic guidelines for using the three senses: sight, smell and taste.

SIGHT

First, look at the colour. It gives clues to its character and what to expect when you taste it. Colour is best seen either by holding the glass in front of a candle or with good daylight or artificial light.

White Wines should be bright and clear. They gain colour with age. As a general rule, the deeper the colour, the more powerful the aroma and taste, either because the wine is fully mature and has gained colour with age, or because it has been made in a much warmer region which accentuates colour, aroma and taste.

There is something wrong with a white wine if it is cloudy or has an unpleasant brown colour.

Sometimes tartrate crystals – like glass or sugar crystals – form in wine, these are unsightly but harmless. They do not taint the wine and quickly fall to the bottom.

Red Wines should also be bright. When they are young, you will see a purple edge which, as the wine ages, changes through plum, brick, mahogany and finally brown, indicating that the wine is at the end of its life. Some red wines are very pale these you can expect to be light in style. Others are dense and opaque, promising a rich, full-bodied wine.

SMELL

Much of the enjoyment of wine is the aroma. Swirl the wine around in the glass and inhale gently. You will be surprised how many flavours this simple process releases, especially if the glass tapers in at the top to concentrate the aromas.

Each grape has its own distinctive smell which you will begin to recognise with practice. Tasting wine is all about association, so, as you sniff the wine, try to find a word that evokes the smell, for example, fruit: raspberries, strawberries, blackcurrants, gooseberries, even more exotic fruits like lychees. Some have a more vegetal smell, others again invoke memories: wood fires, smoke, toast, herbs, spices, even tea.

The important thing is to find a word that conjures up the smell when you taste something similar. What is important is that it means something to you.

TASTE

To get the full benefit from the taste, take a small sip of wine and roll it around your mouth before swallowing. This helps it to touch all the taste buds and reveals many hidden depths.

You will find a fascinating collection of tastes – the basic tastes of fruit, acidity (white wines) and tannin (red wines) – see p.200. With experience, you will also recognise the flavour of oak when wines have been matured in these barrels.

If one element stands out too strongly, ask why. If a red wine is too tannic, for example, it may be too young. If a white wine is too sharp and acidic, it is probably because the grapes were unripe. Often, strong elements soften with age.

When you have drunk the wine, think about the taste left in your mouth. Some wines linger for a long time, others stop short. The more interesting the wine, the more attractive the end-taste. Balance is the key to a pleasing glass of wine.

When comparing wines, you may find the first wine disapppointing. This could be because your taste buds are not yet accustomed to the first assaults of tannin or acidity. This is quite normal and it is certainly worth tasting the first wine again. If you still do not like it, you may well not like the particular grape variety. In which case we show you the names to avoid on the shelves and in the wine lists.

SAUVIGNON BLANC
WORLDWIDE & THE LOIRE

KNOW YOUR GRAPE

SAUVIGNON BLANC – WORLDWIDE & THE LOIRE

Sauvignon Blanc produces the second most fashionable dry white wines in the world today. The grape name never appears on the labels of the most famous bottles from the Loire Valley – Sancerre and Pouilly Fumé (not to be confused with Pouilly Fuissé from Burgundy).

It grows best, and is most characteristic, in the world's coolest vineyard areas; notably the Loire, in France, and New Zealand's South Island. Here, acidity levels are high and the wines are crisp. As the climate gets warmer, the wines lose their acidity but are higher in alcohol and take on a less aggressive character. It is up to you which you prefer.

FLAVOURS

(GOOSEBERRIES)   (GRASSY)

Sauvignon Blanc has a strong, one-dimensional character, providing very dry, crisp and tingly fresh wines, with a pungent aroma and noticeable acidity. Grassy, herbaceous flavours, with strong gooseberry taste. The very marked acidity is pleasing for some but too much for others. It is the acidity which makes Sauvignon Blanc so valuable as a blending wine.

STYLE

ALWAYS DRY

LIGHT	MEDIUM	FULL
✔	✔	✘

IS THE GRAPE NAME ON THE LABEL?

Yes, except Loire Valley, France. Sometimes known as Fumé Blanc. See MAKE THE GRAPE CONNECTION *(p.22)*.

IS IT OAK-AGED?

Some wines – Pouilly Fumé in France and those called Fumé Blanc elsewhere – can be matured in oak for a short while, slightly softening the natural sharpness.

IS IT EVER BLENDED WITH OTHER GRAPES?

Yes, mainly in Bordeaux, where its high acidity gives 'snap' to wines which would otherwise be too bland or flabby. See SÉMILLON *(p.91)*.

HOW MUCH WILL IT COST?

Mostly **A–C**

WHEN TO DRINK

Young and fresh.

KNOW YOUR STYLE

STYLOMETER

LIGHT

NEW ZEALAND	**South Island**	Canterbury, Marlborough, Nelson
FRANCE	**Burgundy**	St Bris
	Loire Valley	Haut Poitou, Touraine
ITALY	**Trentino Alto-Adige**	
	Friuli	
FRANCE	**Loire Valley**	Sancerre, Reuilly, Quincy, Menetou-Salon

MEDIUM

FRANCE	**Loire Valley**	Pouilly Fumé
	South West	Bergerac, Bordeaux, Gaillac, Buzet, Duras
NEW ZEALAND	**North Island**	Auckland, Hawke's Bay, Gisborne
AUSTRALIA	**Victoria**	
	Western Australia	Margaret River
EASTERN EUROPE	**Bulgaria**	
	Hungary	
	Romania	
	Slovenia	
USA	**California**	Monterey, Southern Sonoma, Southern Napa
CHILE	**Maipo Valley**	
	Curico	
USA	**Washington State**	Yakima Valley
SOUTH AFRICA	**Stellenbosch**	
	Franshoek	
	Constantia	
AUSTRALIA	**South Australia**	Barossa, Clare, McLaren Vale

MAKE THE GRAPE CONNECTION

SAUVIGNON BLANC – WORLDWIDE & THE LOIRE

LABELLED BY GRAPE

AUSTRALIA
BULGARIA
CHILE
FRANCE
Bergerac
Bordeaux
Côtes de Buzet
Côtes de Duras
Gaillac
Haut Poitou
St Bris
Touraine
HUNGARY
ITALY
NEW ZEALAND
ROMANIA
SLOVENIA
SOUTH AFRICA
UNITED STATES
California
Washington State

LABELLED BY REGION

FRANCE
Loire Valley
Menetou-Salon
Pouilly-Fumé
Quincy
Reuilly
Sancerre

For lovers of French Sauvignon Blanc, these are the regional names to remember, as the label never shows the grape. For those who dislike Sauvignon Blanc's high acidity, these are obviously the names to avoid.

PLAYING THE GAME

Sauvignon Blanc is always dry. It has achieved a cult, almost snob, appeal under the name Sancerre. One of the more expensive wines it is often too crisp for many people's taste. How many genuinely enjoy its crisp flavour, or know that it is made from 100% Sauvignon Blanc? There are other less expensive styles readily available on wine lists and on the shelves.

Game One
Sauvignon Blanc

Why not serve two Sauvignon Blancs over a meal? Labels masked, of course.
Two good contrasts are a Sancerre, from France, and a Sauvignon Blanc from Chile,
where the grapes are riper and the acidity less noticeable.

Light
Crisp

Medium
Less Crisp

v

Sancerre
Loire, France

Chile
Maipo Valley or Curico

A–B   Up to 2 years; both from the same vintage

If you prefer the Sancerre style and flavour, there are excellent and less expensive alternatives shown in WHAT'S ON THE SHELVES *(p.25)*.

Game Two

Sauvignon Blanc is widely used for blending with the Sémillon grape in Bordeaux. It adds flavour and bite to the much blander Sémillon and its underlying acidity becomes less noticeable. The blended wine should have a more complex taste.

Blended

Entre-Deux-Mers or **White Graves**
Bordeaux, France
(choose a wine with no grape name on the label)

100% Sauvignon Blanc

V **White Bordeaux**
Bergerac or **Côtes de Duras**,
France
(choose wines labelled 'Sauvignon Blanc' or 'Sauvignon Sec')

 A–B ▮◀▬▬ as before

Game Three
Sauvignon Blanc

Sometimes the acidity in Sauvignon Blanc is masked by oak-ageing. It is a different style of wine, less austere and with less gooseberry flavour. Which do you prefer?

Unoaked

New Zealand
Marlborough
or
France
Loire, Touraine

Oak-aged

Pouilly-Fumé
Loire, France
or
USA, New Zealand or **Chile**
Fumé Blanc

V

B–C ▮◀▬▬ up to 2 years; both from the same vintage

What's On The Shelves

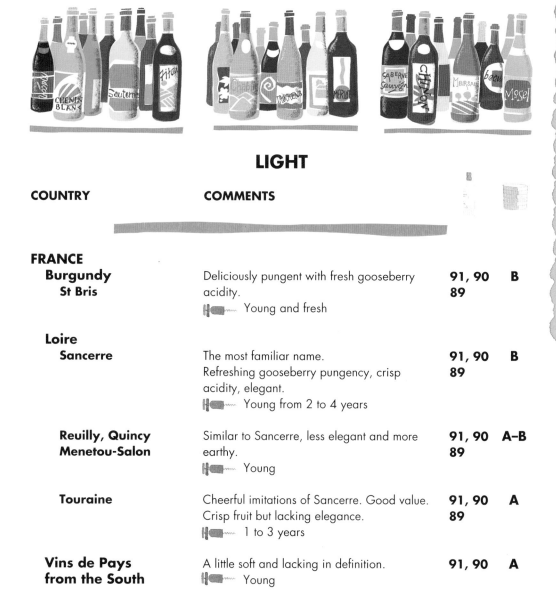

LIGHT

COUNTRY	COMMENTS		
FRANCE			
Burgundy	Deliciously pungent with fresh gooseberry	**91, 90**	**B**
St Bris	acidity.	**89**	
	Young and fresh		
Loire			
Sancerre	The most familiar name.	**91, 90**	**B**
	Refreshing gooseberry pungency, crisp	**89**	
	acidity, elegant.		
	Young from 2 to 4 years		
Reuilly, Quincy	Similar to Sancerre, less elegant and more	**91, 90**	**A–B**
Menetou-Salon	earthy.	**89**	
	Young		
Touraine	Cheerful imitations of Sancerre. Good value.	**91, 90**	**A**
	Crisp fruit but lacking elegance.	**89**	
	1 to 3 years		
Vins de Pays	A little soft and lacking in definition.	**91, 90**	**A**
from the South	Young		
ITALY			
Friuli-Venezia-Giulia	Light, fresh, clean. Attractive, pungent	**91, 90**	**A–B**
Trentino Alto-Adige	flavours from best producers.		
	Within 3 years		

SAUVIGNON BLANC – WORLDWIDE & THE LOIRE

COUNTRY	COMMENTS		
NEW ZEALAND			
South Island	Most exciting Sauvignon Blanc outside France.	91, 90	B–C
Canterbury	Marlborough is considered the best area.	89	
Marlborough	Concentrated fruit, grassy, herbaceous, with		
	firm acidity.		
	⊩⟿ Within 3 or 4 years		

MEDIUM

COUNTRY	COMMENTS		
AUSTRALIA			
South Australia	Climate generally too warm for this variety.	91, 90	B–C
Victoria	Cool areas produce some pungent varietal	89	
Western Australia	character, often similar to Sémillon in		
	Western Australia.		
	⊩⟿ As young as possible		
CHILE		91, 90	A–B
Central Valley		89	
from Maipo	Good varietal character.		
to Curico	⊩⟿ Young		
EASTERN EUROPE			
Bulgaria	Fresh and clean. Inexpensive.	✘	A
Hungary	Fresh, clean, no pronounced varietal taste.		A
Romania	Somewhat dull.		A
Slovenia	Fullness and roundness from a warm climate.		A
	⊩⟿ As young as possible		
FRANCE		90, 89	A–D
Bergerac	In Bordeaux, top white Graves wines may be		
Bordeaux	predominantly Sauvignon Blanc with		
Côtes de Buzet	Sémillon added. Bigger, less refined than		
Côtes de Duras	Loire; earthy.		
	⊩⟿ As young as possible; top Graves		
	from 4 years		

COUNTRY	COMMENTS		
FRANCE **Loire** **Pouilly Fumé**	Some oak ageing is used on top wines. Model for Fumé Blanc around the world. Fuller, softer fruit than Sancerre. ▮▬▬ Before 6 years, the younger the better	**90, 89** **88, 87**	**B**

NEW ZEALAND
North Island
   Auckland
   Gisborne
   Hawke's Bay
	Good varietal character and fuller wines than
	South Island. Fumé Blanc style infers oak-
	ageing, so rounded, buttery with pungent
	gooseberry flavours. Oak-ageing reduces
	flavours and softens acidity.
	▮▬▬ 1 to 4 years
		91, 90
		89
			B–C

SOUTH AFRICA **Constantia** **Franshoek** **Stellenbosch**	Full, clean-tasting. Best have crisp gooseberry flavour, good acidity. ▮▬▬ Young and fresh	**91, 90** **89**	**A–B**

USA
California
   Monterey
   South Napa
   South Sonoma
	The term Fumé Blanc was invented here to
	denote some oak-ageing and a full style.
	Less obvious gooseberry, firm acidity.
	▮▬▬ 2 to 5 years
		90, 89
		87
			A–C

Washington State **Yakima Valley**	Good varietal character. ▮▬▬ Before 5 years	**90, 89** **88**	**A–C**

SAUVIGNON BLANC – WORLDWIDE & THE LOIRE

RELIABLE PRODUCERS & SHIPPERS

LIGHT

FRANCE
Loire
Haut-Poitou: Cave Cooperative de Haut-Poitou
Menetou-Salon: Domaine de Chatenay, Foumier, Henri Pelle, Jean-Max Roger, Le Petit Clos
Quincy: Domaine de la Maison Blanche, Duc de Berri, Meunier, Raymond Pipet
Reuilly: Claude Lafond, Didier Martin
Sancerre: Bernard Bailly-Reverdy, Domaine Thomas et Fils, Domaine Vacheron, Gitton Père et Fils, Jean-Max Roger, Jean Reverdy et Fils, Lucien Crochet, Paul Millerioux, Paul Prieur, Vincent Delaporte
Touraine: Comte d'Ormont, Confrèrie des Vignerons de Oisly et Thésée, Domaine Guenault, Domaine Octavie, Domaine de la Renaudie, Guy Mardon, Guy Saget

ITALY
Alto-Adige: Alois Lageder, Kellereigenossenschaft St Michael, Kellereigenossenschaft Tramin, Kettmeir, Santa Margherita
Friuli: Gravner, Jermann, Livio Felluga, Pighin, Russiz Superiore, Volpe Pasini

NEW ZEALAND
Cloudy Bay, Hunters, Montana, Redwood Valley, Stoneleigh Vineyards

MEDIUM

AUSTRALIA
Delatite, Hardy's, Hill-Smith, Jim Barry, Lindeman, Middlebrook, Taltarni, Wirra Wirra

CHILE
Caliterra, Concha y Toro, Santa Digna, Torres, Villa Montes

EASTERN EUROPE
Bulgarian Vintners Co., Romanian Monopoly

FRANCE
Loire
Pouilly-Fumé: Ch de Nozet, Ch de Tracy, Didier Dagueneau, Domaine de Petit Soumard, Gitton Père et Fils, Guy Saget, Jean Pabiot, Masson-Blondelet, Michel Bailly, Michel Redde,

NEW ZEALAND
Babich, Brookfields, Coopers Creek, Delegats, Morton Estate, Nobilo, Selaks, Vidal, Villa Maria

SOUTH AFRICA
Backsberg, Buitenverwachtung, De Wetshof, Delheim, Klein Constantia, La Motte, Le Bonneur, Stellenryck, Thelema Mountain Vineyards

USA
California: Belvedere, Ch St Jean, Dry Creek, Fetzer, Mondavi, Monticello, Newton Vineyards, William Wheeler, Woodbridge
Washington State: Ch Ste Michelle

CHENIN BLANC
WORLDWIDE & THE LOIRE

KNOW YOUR GRAPE

Chenin Blanc is one of the most versatile grapes, producing dry, medium dry and sweet white wines. However, while Sauvignon Blanc and Chardonnay dominate the fashion stakes, Chenin Blanc remains in the shadows. Quite why this should be is difficult to understand as, on the Loire, the medium dry and sweet white wines can be amongst the finest in the world. Perhaps it is because they are often drunk too young for the full potential of this grape variety to develop and so be appreciated.

FLAVOURS

APPLES   APRICOTS   FRUIT SALAD   HONEY

The driest French wines have a crisp apple flavour, others more of fresh fruit. The steely, crisp apple flavour of French, dry Loire wines is aggressive when young but softens with age and becomes honey-like. Sweeter wines have a delicious honeyed richness, more pronounced when affected with 'noble rot' *(see p.204)*. Chenin Blanc is for those who enjoy its natural high acidity, special freshness and clean taste. When sweet, the acidity sets it apart from the cloying character of so many better known 'pudding' wines, giving them freshness and a long life.

STYLE

DRY   MEDIUM   SWEET
✔   ✔   ✔

From searingly dry to luscious and sweet, usually quite full-bodied. They improve immeasurably with age. The sweet wines are very long-lived.

IS THE GRAPE NAME ON THE LABEL?

Yes, but rarely in France
See MAKE THE GRAPE
CONNECTION *(p.32)*

HOW MUCH WILL IT COST?

A–D

Mostly **B–C**.

IS IT OAK-AGED?

In the Loire Valley the fine, sweet wines of Coteaux du Layon and some of the long-lived, dry wines of Savennières are matured – and in some cases fermented – in oak barrels.

WHEN TO DRINK

Drink the driest when young and fresh. Generally Chenin Blanc improves out of all recognition with age.

IS IT EVER BLENDED WITH OTHER GRAPES?

Occasionally in South Africa.

KNOW YOUR STYLE

STYLOMETER

DRY

FRANCE	**Loire Valley**	Jasnières, Savennières, Anjou Sec, Saumur Sec, Montlouis Sec, Vouvray Sec
NEW ZEALAND	**North Island**	Gisborne, Hawke's Bay

MEDIUM

FRANCE	**Loire Valley**	Anjou Demi-sec, Vouvray Demi-sec, Montlouis Demi-sec
USA	**California**	Napa Valley, Sonoma
	Washington State	Yakima Valley
SOUTH AFRICA	**Paarl** **Robertson** **Stellenbosch**	
AUSTRALIA	**South Australia** **Victoria**	McLaren Vale

SWEET

FRANCE	**Loire Valley**	Coteaux du Layon, Bonnezeaux, Quarts de Chaume, Vouvray
USA	**California**	Central Valley (labelled 'Late Harvest')
SOUTH AFRICA	**Paarl** **Stellenbosch** **Robertson**	(labelled 'Late Harvest' or 'Special Late Harvest')

MAKE THE GRAPE CONNECTION

As with most French wines, Chenin Blanc is labelled by the region. Confusingly and frustratingly, the label does not even tell you whether the bottle you have chosen is dry, medium or sweet.

LABELLED BY GRAPE

AUSTRALIA
Mainly medium dry but a few sweet 'noble rot' wines.
See WINEMAKING *(p.201)*.

CALIFORNIA
Some sweet wines can be found in specialist outlets. These will be called 'Late Harvest'.

NEW ZEALAND
Mainly dry wines available in UK.

SOUTH AFRICA
Often labelled under the South African synonym 'Steen'. Will be called 'Late' or 'Special Late Harvest' when sweet.

LABELLED BY REGION

FRANCE
Loire Valley

DRY
(sometimes labelled as 'sec')
Anjou
Jasnières
Montlouis
Saumur
Savennières
Vouvray

MEDIUM
(sometimes labelled as 'demi-sec')
Anjou
Montlouis
Vouvray

SWEET
(sometimes labelled as 'moelleux')
Bonnezeaux
Coteaux du Layon
Quarts de Chaume
Vouvray

Récolte 1985
CHATEAU DE L'ECHARDERIE

Quarts de Chaume

APPELLATION QUARTS DE CHAUME CONTRÔLÉE

Mis en bouteille au Château

S.C.A. LAFFOURCADE   ROCHEFORT-S/-LOIRE
Propriétaire   (Maine-&-Loire)

PRODUCE OF FRANCE   e 75 cl

PLAYING THE GAME

Three Different Styles for a Summer's Day lawrence

Here is a grape that covers the taste spectrum, from dry to lusciously sweet. Chenin Blanc is one of those rare grapes which you could serve with every course.

THE MENU

STARTER

Wines with good acidity survive a squeeze of lemon or a vinegary dressing, so try Vouvray Sec.

FISH
(not smoked or crabmeat)
or
LIGHT MEAT

DESSERT

(preferably not with apples, because of the appley flavour of Chenin Blanc)

SOFT CHEESES

Chenin Blanc's acidity and sweetness cut through the cheeses' acidity

THE WINES

DRY

Vouvray Sec
2 years
or, for a fine wine
Savennières
4 years +

MEDIUM

For a slightly fuller wine, choose one from a warm climate
South Africa or **USA**, California
4 years

SWEET

Quarts de Chaume, France
or **South Africa**, Edelkeur
or **USA**, California, Late Harvest
 Choose the oldest wines you can find preferably not less than 5 years. Dessert wines improve dramatically with age

WHAT'S ON THE SHELVES

DRY
'sec'

COUNTRY	COMMENTS		
FRANCE			
Loire			
Savennières	Driest most stylish of French Chenin Blancs.	**90, 89**	**B–C**
Coulée de Serrant	Steely acidity when young which develops	**88, 86**	
Clos de la Roche	into more complex, honeyed flavours.	**85**	
	From 4 years but they keep happily for 8 to 10 years. They age brilliantly		
Anjou Sec	Quite steely, almost mouthwateringly green,	**90, 89**	**A–B**
Jasnières	in first 3 to 4 years. Develop more subtle	**88**	
Montlouis Sec	flavours with age.		
Saumur Sec	3 to 5 years		
Vouvray Sec			
NEW ZEALAND			
North Island	Most exciting Chenin Blancs outside France.	**91, 90**	**B–C**
Gisborne	Wonderful fruit salad flavours with a touch	**89**	
Hawke's Bay	of honey and balanced acidity.		
Henderson	3 to 5 years		

MEDIUM
'demi sec'

FRANCE			
Loire			
Anjou Blanc	Anjou Blanc is undistinguished, often	**90, 89**	**B–C**
Montlouis	over-acidic. Vouvray and Montlouis produce	**88, 86**	
Vouvray	delicate, honeyed wines with apricot flavour. Good acidity.	**85, 83**	
	Can be drunk young but best from 3 to 5 years		

COUNTRY	COMMENTS		
SOUTH AFRICA **Paarl**	Soft, fruity, with less honey and acidity than Loire. ⏲ Before 5 years	**91, 90** **89**	**A–B**

USA
California
  Napa Valley
  Sonoma
	The wines lack high acidity of French Chenin. Varietal character with honey and melon flavour.
	⏲ 1 to 3 years
		90	**B**

Washington State **Yakima Valley**	Fresh fruit and honey flavours. ⏲ Young and fresh	**90**	**B**
AUSTRALIA **South Australia** **McLaren Vale** **Victoria**	Mainly used for easy-quaffing, boxed wine. Bland, low in acidity. ⏲ As young as possible	**91, 90**	**A–B**

SWEET
'moelleux' or 'doux'

FRANCE
Loire
  Bonnezeaux
  Coteaux du Layon
  Quarts de Chaume
  Vouvray
	Some of the greatest French sweet wines. Finest are Bonnezeaux and Quarts de Chaume. Concentrated, superb rich honeyed apricot flavour with high acidity to prevent any cloying taste.
	⏲ At their best from 5 years – up to 20 and more from best vintages
		90, 89
		88, 85
		or any
		older
		you
		can
		find!
			B–D

USA **California** **Central Valley**	Sweet, honeyed wines lacking a little acidity. ⏲ 3 to 8 years	**90, 88** **87, 86** **85**	**B–C**
SOUTH AFRICA **Paarl** **Robertson** **Stellenbosch**	Rich, honeyed wines with less acidity than Loire wines. ⏲ 3 to 10 years	**91, 90** **88, 86,** **85**	**B–C**

35

CHENIN BLANC – WORLDWIDE & THE LOIRE

RELIABLE SHIPPERS & PRODUCERS

DRY

FRANCE
Savennières: Clos de la Coulée-de-Serrant, Clos du Papillon (props. Baumard & Mme de Jessy), Domaine de la Bizolière, Domaine Roches aux Moines, Domaine du Closel, Yves Soulez

Vouvray Sec: Bertier-Pichot, Ch Moncontour, Foreau, Huet, Jean-Baptiste Pinon, Marc Bredif, Poniatowski

NEW ZEALAND
Collards, Cooks, Matawhero

SWEET

FRANCE
Ch Bellerive, Ch de Fesles, Ch de Plaisance, Ch du Suronde, Domaine de Baumard, Domaine de Lamotte, Domaine de la Soucherie, Domaine des Hauts-Perrays, Rene Renou

SOUTH AFRICA
Delheim, de Wetshof, Nederburg 'Edelkur'

USA
California: Dry Creek

MEDIUM

AUSTRALIA
Berri Estate, Coriole, Houghton, Peel Estate, Tollana

FRANCE
Vouvray/Montlouis: Berger Frères, Brault Père et Fils, Ch de Valliennes, Ch Moncontour, Domaine Richou, Dominique Moyer, Foreau, G Deletang, Huet, Marc Bredif, Poniatowski

SOUTH AFRICA
Boschendal, KWV

USA
California: Christian Brothers, Dry Creek, Hacienda, J Lohr

RIESLING
WORLDWIDE

FAMOUS REGIONS: RHEIN & MOSEL, GERMANY

KNOW YOUR GRAPE

Riesling is a white grape which prospers in the cooler wine regions and is now grown worldwide. The best wines come from Germany where they are at their most complex, as are the labels. The styles are so varied, from very dry to luscious and sweet, that somewhere in the world there may well be a Riesling that will suit your own particular taste.

The name Riesling is wrongly attached to unrelated and lesser varieties – the Riesling Italico of Italy, the Laski Riesling of Slovenia, the Olasz Riesling of Hungary and the Cape Riesling of South Africa. It is also wrongly linked to Liebfraumilch – a made-up name for usually very ordinary and sometimes downright poor German wines which seldom contain Riesling.

FLAVOURS

SLATE · LEMONS · PEACHES · PINEAPPLES · PASSION FRUIT · HONEY

Fresh and floral, with a huge range of aromatic, grapy flavours. With maturity, the smell is reminiscent of petrol! Surprisingly, not unattractive. Riesling's naturally high acidity produces a refreshing, crisp style of dry wine and provides essential balance in sweet wines. Unlike most other grapes, acidity levels do not decrease as wines get sweeter, so even the richest dessert wines have a fresh, crisp taste that prevents them from becoming cloying.

STYLE

DRY ✔   **MEDIUM** ✔   **SWEET** ✔

Varies from the driest in Alsace and Australia to the sweetest dessert wines of Germany, Austria, Australia and USA. Good wines are balanced between fruitiness and acidity.

WHEN TO DRINK

Drink the lightest and freshest as young as possible. Alsace Rieslings and the richer, sweeter wines will improve with keeping from 4 years onwards.

IS IT EVER BLENDED WITH OTHER GRAPES?

Occasionally in Australia and New Zealand, with Sauvignon Blanc or Gewürztraminer. The label will always tell you.

IS IT OAK-AGED?

Oak rarely gives any benefit to Riesling, so most come from tanks.

HOW MUCH WILL IT COST?

A–D

As a general guide, the sweeter and richer the wines, the higher the price.

IS THE GRAPE NAME ON THE LABEL?

Almost always, but sometimes with a local prefix. See MAKE THE GRAPE CONNECTION (p.40).

KNOW YOUR STYLE

STYLOMETER
(Quality in brackets)

DRY

NEW ZEALAND	**South Island**	Christchurch, Marlborough, Central Otago, Canterbury
GERMANY	**Mosel & Rhein**	
ITALY	**Trentino Alto-Adige, Friuli-Venezia-Giulia**	
AUSTRALIA	**South Australia**	Pewsey Vale, Clare, Eden Valley
AUSTRIA	**Niederöstereich**	(Kabinett quality)
FRANCE	**Alsace**	(Grand Cru)

MEDIUM

FRANCE	**Alsace**	(Vendange Tardive)
GERMANY	**Mosel & Rhein**	(Halbtrocken or Spätlese)
USA	**California**	Monterey, Sonoma
AUSTRIA	**Wachau**	(Spätlese quality)
USA	**Oregon, Washington State**	
AUSTRALIA	**South Australia**	Barossa Valley, Clare, Eden Valley, Southern Vales
SOUTH AFRICA	**Stellenbosch**	(Late Harvest)

SWEET

FRANCE	**Alsace**	('Sélection de grains nobles')
GERMANY	**Mosel & Rhein**	(Auslese, Beerenauslese, Trockenbeerenauslese)
AUSTRALIA	**South Australia**	(Late Harvest)
NEW ZEALAND	**South Island**	(Late Harvest)
AUSTRIA	**Wachau**	As for Germany
USA	**California, Oregon, Washington State**	(Late Harvest, Select Late Harvest, Special Select Late Harvest)
SOUTH AFRICA	**Stellenbosch**	(Special Late Harvest)

MAKE THE GRAPE CONNECTION

Riesling always appears on the label but sometimes under a synonym

COUNTRY	LABELLED AS
AUSTRIA	Rheinriesling or Weisser (white) Riesling
AUSTRALIA	Rhine Riesling
FRANCE **Alsace**	Riesling d'Alsace
GERMANY	Riesling
ITALY	Riesling Renano or Rheinriesling
NEW ZEALAND	Rhine Riesling
SOUTH AFRICA	Weisser (white) Riesling
USA **California**	Johannisberg Riesling or White Riesling
Oregon **Washington State**	White Riesling
	Johannisberg Reisling or White Riesling for sweet wines

Riesling labels will also give an indication of the *levels* of sweetness

DRY

COUNTRY

GERMANY & AUSTRIA
(follows German system of classification)
see RIESLING – GERMANY *(p.47)*

FRANCE
Alsace
For the three classifications see
GEWURZTRAMINER *(p.57)*. 'Vendange
Tardive' (Late Harvest) does not
necessarily mean that the wine is sweet;
but it will have more weight and alcohol
than straightforward Riesling

SWEET

COUNTRY	LABELLED AS
GERMANY & AUSTRIA see RIESLING – GERMANY *(p.47)*	
FRANCE **Alsace**	'Sélection de grains nobles'
NEW ZEALAND, AUSTRALIA & USA	Sweet dessert wines called in ascending order 'Late Harvest', 'Select Late Harvest', 'Special Select Late Harvest' or 'Noble Late Harvest'
SOUTH AFRICA	'Special Late Harvest'

PLAYING THE GAME

Lawrence

Game One
Imposter v The Real McCoy

Riesling's reputation suffers from its erroneous association with Liebfraumilch – a sugary alcoholic drink with little character and no Riesling. Hopefully, you will taste the difference. Why not try both with labels masked?

The Imposter

The Real McCoy
100% Resling

Liebfraumilch
any

v

Kabinett Riesling
Rhein, Germany
For fair comparison not Trocken (dry)
or Halb-Trocken (semi dry)

A–B   Select wines from the same vintage – up to 2 years

41

Game Two
Riesling

Another hurdle Riesling must overcome is the belief that it is always sweet. In fact in Alsace and Australia it is traditionally dry. The Germans, too, now make dry Rieslings (labelled 'Trocken'). So why not compare dry and medium dry styles?

Dry

Alsace
or
Australia
South Australia, Rhine Riesling
or
Germany
Riesling Trocken

Medium

Germany
Rhein, Kabinett or Spätlese

A–B Different harvesting times, so choose 3 years from France or Germany, 2 years from Australia

Game Three
Dessert Wines

Many of the world's greatest dessert wines are made from Riesling. Fortunately often found in half bottles as they are invariably expensive and a little can go a very long way.

Sweet

Germany or **Austria**
Auslese
or
USA or **New Zealand**
Late Harvest

Sweeter

Germany or **Austria**
Beerenauslese or
Trockenbeerenauslese (the sweeter)
or
South Africa or **Australia**
Special Late Harvest

B–D 5 years plus, and see how sweet your tooth is!

Riesling should be tasted chilled but not frozen. The sweeter the wine, the more you may chill it without doing too much harm but the sweetness is less obvious.

WHAT'S ON THE SHELVES

DRY

COUNTRY	COMMENTS		
AUSTRALIA			
South Australia	Floral, delicate, with added citric flavour.	**91, 90**	**A–B**
Clare	Traditionally dry, with full, overt taste of	**88**	
Eden Valley	pineapple and passion fruit.		
Pewsey Vale	⌐══ 2 to 5 years		
AUSTRIA			
Niederöstereich	Firm, with long, floral flavour, less acidity	**91, 90**	**B**
	and more alcohol than German Rieslings.	**89**	
	⌐══ 2 to 5 years		
FRANCE			
Alsace	Very dry, with steely edge, developing	**90, 89**	**A–C**
	characteristic petrolly aroma with age.	**88, 86**	
	Minimum alcohol level 11°.	**85, 83**	
	⌐══ Least expensive from 3 years. The best will mature for a further 4 to 5 years or more		
GERMANY	See RIESLING – GERMANY (p.47)		
NEW ZEALAND			
South Island	Worth watching out for. Delicate, fresh wines,	**91, 90**	**A–B**
Canterbury	with strong varietal character and excellent	**89**	
Central Otago	balance of acidity and fruit.		
Christchurch	⌐══ Young and fresh, 2 to 4 years		
Marlborough			

MEDIUM

COUNTRY	COMMENTS		

AUSTRALIA
South Australia
  Barossa Valley
  Clare
  Eden Valley
  Southern Vales
	More off-dry than medium dry, with lemony flavour. Barossa has more weight and less elegance than wines of Eden Valley and Pewsey Vale.
	2 to 5 years
		91, 90
		88
			A–B

AUSTRIA **Niederöstereich**	Kabinett and Spätlese qualities with good varietal character. 3 to 6 years	91, 90 89, 88 87	B–C
FRANCE **Alsace**	In very warm years 'Vendange Tardive' (Late Harvest) wines are medium dry to sweet. Rich, concentrated fruit, higher alcohol. 3 years, but will continue to improve for another 10 or so	90, 89 88, 86 85, 83	C
GERMANY	See RIESLING – GERMANY (p.47)		
ITALY **Friuli-Venezia-Giulia**	Fuller, sometimes rather flabby and dull when lacking acidity. Exciting quality among more expensive bottles. Will improve up to 5 years. Drink less expensive within 2 years	90, 89 87	B–C
Trentino Alto-Adige	Light, elegant, just off-dry, with a slight 'spritz' and lively freshness. Young and fresh	90, 89	B

SOUTH AFRICA
  Paarl
  Robertson
  Stellenbosch
	Fairly rare in UK. Good varietal character Quite full-bodied, low in acidity, tend towards blandness.
	2 to 4 years
		91, 90
		89
			B

COUNTRY	COMMENTS		
USA			
California **Monterey** **Sonoma**	Clean fruit flavours, high in alcohol, good acidity. German style and flavour but with more weight. 2 to 5 years	90, 89	B–C
Oregon **Washington State**	Riesling is new to the Pacific North West where it has exciting potential. Medium dry to medium sweet. More elegant than California, more alcohol than in Germany, medium acidity and good German-style fruit. 2 to 4 years	91, 90 89	A–B

SWEET

FRANCE **Alsace**	'Sélection de grains nobles' made in exceptionally hot years only. Rich and strong, with concentrated fruit, but still French in style. 5 to 10 years or more	90, 89 88, 86 85, 83	D
GERMANY	See Riesling – Germany (p.47).		
NEW ZEALAND **South Island** **Canterbury** **Nelson**	'Late Harvest' A few superb 'noble rot' dessert wines. Rich, fragrant, with ripe fruit and balanced acidity. 3 to 8 years	91, 90 89, 88	B–C
SOUTH AFRICA **Stellenbosch**	Rare 'noble rot' dessert wines labelled 'Special Late Harvest'. Very rich, honeyed, low acidity. 5 to 10 years	87, 86 85	B
USA **California** **Napa Valley**	Rich, honeyed, lemony fruit. High alcohol heavyweights with fair acidity. 5 to 8 years	90, 89 88, 87	B–D
Washington State	'Late Harvest' wines. Honeyed, rich fruit. 5 to 8 years	90, 89 88, 87	B–D

RELIABLE PRODUCERS & SHIPPERS

DRY

AUSTRALIA
Hardy, Heggies, Hill-Smith, Jeffrey Grosset, Jim Barry, Lindemans, Mitchell, Stanley Leasingham, Tim Knappstein, Wynns, Yalumba

AUSTRIA
Fritz Salomon, Lenz Moser, Metternich Weinguter, Schloss Gobelsburg, Winzergenossenschaft Wachau

FRANCE
Alsace: Caves de Bennwihr, Caves des Vignerons de Turckheim, Domaine Ostertag, Dopff au Moulin, Dopff et Irion, Gustave Lorentz, Hugel, J Becker, Jos Meyer, Kuentz-Bas, Leon Beyer, Rolly Gassmann, Theo Faller, Schlumberger, Trimbach, Willm, Willy Gisselbrecht, Zind-Humbrecht

ITALY
Alto Adige, Friuli: Jermann, Kellereigenossenschaft Girlan, Tiefenbrunner

SOUTH AFRICA
Buitenverwachting, Delheim, de Wetshof, Klein Constantia, Nederberg, Simonsig, Zevenwacht

MEDIUM

FRANCE
Alsace: A & O Muré, Dopff au Moulin, Hugel, Kuentz-Bas, Louis Gisselbrecht, Pierre Sparr, Rolly Gassman, Schlumberger, Theo Faller, Zind-Humbrecht

NEW ZEALAND
Giesen, Martinborough Vineyard, Millton Vineyard, Montana, Redwood Valley Estates (Seifried Estate), St Helena

SOUTH AFRICA
Backsberg, Boschendal, Groot Constantia, KWV, Simonsig

USA
California: Beringer Vineyards, Ch St Jean, Firestone, Freemark Abbey, Jekel, Joseph Phelps, Mark West, Robert Mondavi, Simi, Stag's Leap Wine Cellars, Trefethen, Wente Brothers
Oregon: Elk Cove, The Hogue Cellars, Kiona, Knudsen-Erath
Washington State: Snoqualmie

SWEET

AUSTRALIA
South Australia: Heggies, Pewsey Vale, Thomas Hardy

FRANCE
Alsace: A & O Muré, Dopff au Moulin, Hugel Kuentz-Bas, Leon Beyer, Louis Gisselbrecht, Pierre Sparr, Rolly Gassman, Theo Faller, Zind-Humbrecht

NEW ZEALAND
Giesen, Redwood Valley Estates (Seifried Estate), Rippon Vineyard, Torlesse Wines

SOUTH AFRICA
Nederberg, Simonsig

USA
California: Ch St Jean, Clos du Bois, Freemark Abbey, Jekel, Joseph Phelps, Mark West, Robert Mondavi
Washington State: Ch Ste Michelle

NB For German wine producers see RIESLING – GERMANY *(starts opposite)*.

RIESLING
GERMANY

KNOW YOUR GRAPE

Riesling is the finest of Germany's white grapes, not to be confused with the different and inferior varieties called Laski, Welsch or Olasz Riesling and Riesling Italico. Sadly, most people believe that all German wine is made from Riesling, so its reputation is tarnished by the enormous volume of cheap wine from Germany, e.g. Liebfraumilch. Very little of which is made from Riesling. It is also very hard to choose Riesling because the German wine laws and labels are a minefield. We have done our best to chart a path, but, as German wine labels are so complex, the format of this guide differs from the rest.

Riesling is a marvellously versatile grape, producing wines from very dry to lusciously sweet. All have the wonderful balance of fruit and acidity which gives German Rieslings their elegant and racy style. As they are often low in alcoholic strength, they make perfect wines for summer days.

FLAVOURS

SLATE · SOFT FRUITS · FRUIT SALAD · PEACHES · PINEAPPLES

STYLE

DRY ✔ **MEDIUM** ✔ **SWEET** ✔

High acidity ensures long life, allowing flavours and complexities to develop. Mostly low in alcohol and by law need only achieve 7°. Sweeter wines are stronger (except Beerenauslese and Trockenbeerenauslese) but still usually at least 2° lower than equivalent wines from other countries. Strongest are likely to be Trocken (dry) or Halbtrocken (half dry) wines when all the sugar has been converted into alcohol.

HOW MUCH WILL IT COST?

A–D

Plenty of choice in **A**. **B–C** provide best value for money.

IS IT OAK-AGED?

New oak is rarely used as it would mask Riesling's delicacy. Large, or very large, old oak casks are sometimes used for maturation, as they assist development without imparting flavour.

WHEN TO DRINK

• Lightest and driest: 1 to 2 years to capture fresh and spicy fragrance

• Medium: 3 to 4 years

• Sweetest: 8 to 15 years dependent on the vintage.

IS IT EVER BLENDED WITH OTHER GRAPES?

Occasionally, and then the second grape will be mentioned on the label.

IS THE GRAPE NAME ON THE LABEL?

Yes, but usually buried in a mass of other complicated names.

KNOW YOUR STYLE

THE FIVE MAJOR REGIONS FOR RIESLING

There are 13 wine regions in the new unified Germany specified for Quality wine. This guide covers the five most important for Riesling. Winemakers play a vital role, producing wines in eight styles, from dry to very sweet, light to full bodied, low to high in alcohol. Each region produces every style, whilst retaining its regional characteristics.

Region/Comments	Best known wine names
MOSEL	
Mosel-Saar-Ruwer Delicate, fragrant aroma. Crisp, slaty; soft fruit flavours.	Bernkasteler Graacher Piesporter
RHEIN	
Nahe Almost Mosel-like in Schloss Böckelheim; fuller in Kreuznach.	Kreuznacher Schlossböckelheimer
Pfalz Round, generally fuller than other regions; earthy.	Deidesheimer Dürkheimer Forster
Rheingau Aristocrats of Rhein wines. Rich, fruity; spicy perfume, balanced acidity.	Eltviller Erbacher Hochheimer Johannisberger Oestricher Rüdesheimer
Rheinhessen Soft, easy to drink.	Niersteiner Oppenheimer

SOIL

Soil plays a major part in the taste of German wines. The slate on the Mosel's steep slopes produces delicious slaty flavours with fruity acidity. The red soil in the finest Rheinhessen vineyards gives extra richness. The volcanic soil with its warmer climate in the Pfalz produces rounded wines with lower acidity. The heavy Rheingau soil, on slopes overlooking the Rhein and protected from winds by the Taunus hills, produces steely acidity giving depth of character to older wines.

Know Your Style

THE EIGHT BASIC STYLES

This table gives a very general guide to the styles, as there are so many variations. The winemakers may, if they wish, turn Kabinett, Spätlese and Auslese into dry wines (Trocken or Halbtrocken). They will have higher alcohol levels than the 'normal' styles and may be labelled Kabinett Trocken, Spätlese Trocken, Auslese Trocken, or Halbtrocken as the case may be.

STYLE	DESCRIPTION	COMMENTS
DRY	**Trocken**	Wines with less than 9 grams of residual sugar per litre
	Halbtrocken	Wines with 9 to 18 grams of residual sugar per litre
MEDIUM DRY	**Kabinett**	Light, delicate wines (25+ grams) made from ripe grapes picked at normal harvest time. Grapy and easy to drink.
MEDIUM SWEET	**Spätlese**	(= late picked) Ripe grapes (35+ grams) picked at least seven days later than normal harvest time, producing more natural sugar and flavour than Kabinett wines.
SWEET	**Auslese**	(= selected) (40+ grams) Selected bunches of ripe grapes, producing usually sweet wines with concentrated aroma and taste. Rich and flavoursome.
	(From Auslese level onwards, the winemaker is not allowed to interfere with the sweetness)	
VERY SWEET	**Beerenauslese**	(= single grape selection) Very ripe, individually selected grapes, producing rich, sweet and luscious dessert wines with good acidity to prevent them being cloying.
	Eiswein	(= frozen wine) Grapes of beerenauslese ripeness and richness but left until frozen on the vine, usually late November but sometimes even later. Acidity levels are high so wines last up to 20 years.
	Trockenbeerenauslese	(= selected dried grapes) Small, individually selected, shrivelled almost raisln-like grapes. Rare, occuring only in finest years after perfect, autumn weather. The grapes are always affected by 'noble rot'. Extremely rich and sweet, and, due to the high acidity, will keep for decades.

MAKE THE GRAPE CONNECTION

Once you have decided which style you prefer, you then face the nightmare of German wine labels. At least you can spot the main areas – Mosel-Saar-Ruwer wines are always in green bottles, Rhein wines always in brown.

THE TWO LEVELS OF QUALITY WINE

This is always shown on the label and is coded as follows, QmP being the higher quality:

QmP
'Qualitswein mit Prädikat'
(literally 'Quality wine with distinction')

These include Kabinett, Spätlese, Auslese, Eiswein, Trockenbeerenauslese and Beerenauslese. No sugar may be added to raise alcohol levels.

QbA
'Qualitätswein bestimmter Anbaugebiete'
(literally 'Quality wine from specified areas')

This is basic Quality wine, usually from a not very ripe crop. Sugar may be added before fermentation to raise alcohol to permitted levels. Wines are dry or sweet dependent on the winemaker.

MAKE THE GRAPE CONNECTION

VINEYARD NAMES

There are thousands of vineyard names, so we give a short list *(opposite)* of those you are most likely to see on the wine shelves. All individual Estate bottlings (Einzellage) are produced in smallish quantities and tend to be drier than Grosslage (group of vineyards) wines from the same region which have been bottled in volume and sweetened for a mass market. Einzellagen wines are always QmP; Grosslagen wines are usually QmP but may sometimes be QbA.

Single vineyards (Einzellagen)

The word Einzellage never appears on the label but the vineyard name does, preceded by the village name, e.g. Bernkasteler (village) Doktor (vineyard).

Groups of vineyards (Grosslagen)

When a wine is made from a blend of two or more specified vineyards, it is given a collective name (Grosslage). Grosslage is not shown on the label but the collective name is preceded by the village name, e.g. Bernkasteler (village) Badstube (group of vineyards).

Unfortunately, there is no differentiation on labels between a 'Grosslage' or an 'Einzellage' wine. See list of RELIABLE PRODUCERS & SHIPPERS *(p.56)* for some of the names you are most likely to find in the UK. To cover the full list is a book in itself.

NB: BEREICH (district): bottles labelled 'Bereich' are on most shelves. They must be Quality rating but seldom contain Riesling. The name describes wines made anywhere within the designated vineyard region and is followed by a designated village name, usually the most famous in the area, e.g. 'Bereich Nierstein'.

The style shown on the label, e.g. Kabinett, Spätlese, Auslese – traditionally accepted as medium dry, medium sweet and sweet – may denote something quite different.

Paul Anheu
Weingut · D-6550 Bad Kreuznach

Nahe

1990er
Kreuznacher Kahlenbe
Riesling Spätlese
Qualitätswein mit Prädikat
Amtliche Prüfungsnummer 1 710 0017 021 91

alc 8,0% vol   Erzeugerabfüllung
Produce of Germany

Rathsweinkellerei

Qualitätswein
1991er Bereich Bernkastel
Riesling ·
alc.9%vol   A. P. Nr. 2 606 365 030 92   750 ml
RATHSWEINKELLEREI BECKER

AP. NR. 3561077-24-90
PRODUCE OF
GERMANY

QUALITÄTSWEIN
MIT PRÄDIKAT

Alc. 7.0% vol

750 ml e

MOSEL · SAAR · RUWER

1989 JOSEPHSHÖFER*
RIESLING TROCKENBEERENAUSLESE
ERZEUGERABFÜLLUNG
REICHSGRAF VON KESSELSTATT
D- 5500 TRIER

SINGLE VINEYARDS

REGION	BEST KNOWN SINGLE VINEYARDS
MOSEL	
Mosel-Saar-Ruwer	Bernkasteler Doktor, Graacher Himmelreich, Piesporter Goldtröpfchen, Wehlener Sonnenuhr, Wiltinger Kupp
RHEIN	
Nahe	Kreuznacher Kahlenberg, Schlossböckelheimer Kupfergrube
Pfalz	Forster Jesuitengarten, Wachenheimer Gerümpel
Rheingau	Rüdesheimer Schlossberg, Kiedricher Sandgrub, Winkeler Hasensprung, Hochheimer Königin Victoria Berg, Oestricher Lenchen
Rheinhessen	Niersteiner Findling, Niersteiner Hipping

GROUPS OF VINEYARDS

REGION	BEST KNOWN GROUPS OF VINEYARDS
MOSEL	
Mosel-Saar-Ruwer	Bernkasteler Badstube, Graacher Münzlay, Piesporter Michelsberg, Wiltinger Scharzberg, Zeller Schwarze Katz
RHEIN	
Nahe	Rüdesheimer Rosengarten
Pfalz	Forster Mariengarten, Wachenheimer Mariengarten
Rheingau	Kiedricher Heiligenstock, Hochheimer Daubhaus, Oestricher Gottesthal, Rüdesheimer Burgweg, Winkeler Honigberg
Rheinhessen	Niersteiner Gutes Domthal, Niersteiner Rehbach, Niersteiner Spiegelberg

PLAYING THE GAME

Game One
Riesling

Riesling, in Germany, produces more styles than any other grape in any other part of the world, so the permutations for comparison are countless. A good start is to compare the difference between Mosel and Rhein.

Mosel

Bernkastel
Trocken (dry)
or Halbtrocken (half dry)

v

Rhein

Niersteiner
Trocken (dry)
or Halbtrocken (half dry)

A–B   2 years

Detect the slaty flavours and more noticeable acidity of the Mosel wine compared to the rounder taste of the Niersteiner.

Game Two
Riesling

Now, choose either Mosel or Rhein and compare the different styles. Whichever you choose, be certain to see that the wines are the same region and vintage.

Dry Kabinett Trocken or Kabinett Halbtrocken		Medium Dry Kabinett (NB: These medium dry labels must **not** say Trocken or Halbtrocken)
Bernkasteler or **Zeltinger**		**Bernkasteler** or **Zeltinger**
Schlossböckelheimer Nahe	v	**Schlossböckelheimer** Nahe
Johannisberger Rheingau		**Johannisberger** Rheingau
Niersteiner Rheinhessen		**Niersteiner** Rheinhessen
Deidesheimer Pfalz		**Deidesheimer** Pfalz

B   2 to 3 years

Game Three
Riesling

Medium Sweet	v	Sweet
Spätlese		**Auslese**

B-C   3 to 4 years

If you prefer sweeter styles, they are available in any of the above regions and districts.

RELIABLE PRODUCERS & SHIPPERS

The names of German producers and shippers are nearly as daunting as the names of their wines, so, if you are able to consult a specialist wine merchant, this is the moment to do so (see p.215). Here are a few of the top producers and shippers.

MOSEL-SAAR-RUWER

Mosel: Bischöfliches Konvikt, Dr Loosen, Dr Thanisch, Friedrich Wilhelm Gymnasium, Fritz Haag, J J Prum, Kesselstatt, Priesterseminar, Vereinigte Hospitien, Willi Haag

Saar: Bert Simon, Dr Fischer, Egon Müller, Hohe Domkirche, von Hoevel, von Volxem

Ruwer: Kathäuserhof, von Schubert

RHEIN

Nahe: August Anheuser, Paul Anheuser, Staatsdomaine Niederhausen, von Plettenberg

Pfalz: Basserman-Jordan, Bürklin-Wolf, Josef Biffar, von Buhl

Rheingau: Georg Breuer, H H Eser, Landgraf von Hessen, Molitor, Nägler, Schloss Rheinhartshausen, Schloss Schönborn, Schloss Vollrads, Staatsdomaine Eltville, von Brentano, von Simmern,

Rheinhessen: Anton Balbach, H Braun, Herman Franz Schmitt

GEWÜRZTRAMINER
WORLDWIDE & ALSACE

KNOW YOUR GRAPE

The Gewürztraminer grape, with its distinctive aroma and taste, is easier to identify than most and is made from dry to sweet, though it is mostly dry. The world-wide reputation stems from Alsace.

Gewürztraminer's spicy and aromatic character makes it one of the few wines which complement smoked salmon and Chinese food.

FLAVOURS

(LYCHEES) (MANGOES) (GRAPEFRUIT) (GINGER)

Gewürz means spicy. Dry or sweet, Gewürztraminer is definitely exotic and occasionally almost over the top in its heady, spicy flavour. The outstanding feature of Gewürztraminer is the aroma – aromatic, spicy, sometimes even muscat-like – in short, scented. Acidity levels are good but never pronounced.

STYLE

Always FULL

DRY   MEDIUM   SWEET
✔   ✔   ✔

Like Riesling, Gewürztraminer covers the spectrum from very dry to very sweet. When late picked, the alcohol level is higher than Riesling. The weight and strength increases with the quality and sweetness of the wines.

WHEN TO DRINK

Drink the lightest really young. Most need at least 3 years after the vintage, the best even more.

IS IT OAK-AGED?

Gewürztraminer is not improved by the taste of oak. Where oak vats are used, they are either too old or too large to impart any flavour to the wines.

IS IT EVER BLENDED WITH OTHER GRAPES?

Seldom. The label will always indicate the grapes used for blending.

IS THE GRAPE NAME ON THE LABEL?

Yes, but sometimes under a local variant.

HOW MUCH WILL IT COST?

A–D

Mostly **B–C**. Some wines in the upper end of **A**.

Know Your Style

STYLOMETER

DRY

ITALY	**Trentino Alto-Adige**	
NEW ZEALAND	**South Island**	Canterbury, Otago, Marlborough
FRANCE	**Alsace**	
GERMANY	**Rhein**	Pfalz, Baden (Kabinett wines)
AUSTRIA	**Burgenland, Styria**	
USA	**Oregon**	
FRANCE	**Alsace**	(Grand Cru and most 'Vendange Tardive' wines)

MEDIUM

AUSTRIA	**Burgenland, Styria**	(Spätlese wines)
GERMANY	**Rhein**	Pfalz, Baden (Spätlese wines)
CROATIA	**Kutjevo**	
SLOVENIA	**Lutomer**	
NEW ZEALAND	**North Island**	Gisborne
AUSTRALIA	**South Australia**	
USA	**California**	Mendocino, Napa Valley, Sonoma County
SOUTH AFRICA	**Paarl, Stellenbosch**	
FRANCE	**Alsace**	('Vendange Tardive' wines in exceptional years)

SWEET

NEW ZEALAND	**North Island**	(Late Harvest)
GERMANY	**Rhein**	Pfalz, Baden (Beerenauslese and Trockenbeerenauslese)
AUSTRIA	**Burgenland, Styria**	(Beerenauslese and Trockenbeerenauslese)
FRANCE	**Alsace**	(Sélection de grains nobles – rare)
SOUTH AFRICA	**Paarl, Stellenbosch**	(Late Harvest)
USA	**California**	(Late Harvest)

MAKE THE GRAPE CONNECTION

Some labels show the grape variety – Gewürztraminer – others will show the local name for the grape. The label will often give an indication whether the wine is dry, medium or sweet.

CLASSIFICATION

ALSACE

In Alsace, France, there are three classifications which were recently introduced to add prestige to the best wines. They indicate the style.

GRAND CRU

This designation encompasses 48 of the best vineyard sites, though not necessarily the best producers. The vineyard name and the words 'Grand Cru' always appear on the label. These wines are more complex than straightforward Gewürztraminer when made by the best winemakers, but they are hard to distinguish from the basic wines when made by the rest. See RELIABLE PRODUCERS & SHIPPERS (p.66).

VENDANGE TARDIVE ('Late harvest'):

The equivalent of German 'Spätlese' (late picked) wines but quite unlike them in style. Because of Alsace's tradition of making dry wines, the extra sugar in the grapes from late picking is all converted into alcohol. The wines are thus invariably dry but much higher in alcohol than the basic Gewürztraminer. In exceptional years, when the grapes are super-ripe and some residual sugar is left after fermentation, the wines are medium/dry rather than medium/sweet.

SELECTION DE GRAINS NOBLES ('Selected, very ripe late-picked grapes'):

The equivalent of German Trockenbeerenauslese wines but even the Alsatians cannot turn all the sugar from these super-ripe grapes into alcohol. The minimum potential alcohol allowed is 16.4° but is usually between 19° and 23°, so the wines are both powerful and sweet – often very sweet.

STYLE

All Alsace Gewürztraminer is full. The weight and strength increases with the quality and sweetness of the wines.

STYLE	LABELLED AS
DRY	
(this accounts for over 95% of the Alsace Gewürztraminer on the UK shelves)	
FULL	Gewürztraminer
FULLER	Grand Cru
FULLEST	Vendange Tardive
MEDIUM	
(outstanding years only)	
FULL	Vendange Tardive
SWEET	
(very rare)	
FULL	Sélection de grains nobles

WORLDWIDE

For the rest of the world, the style of Gewürztraminer is labelled as follows:

DRY

AUSTRIA   Gewürztraminer
ITALY
  Trentino Alto-Adige
           Gewürztraminer or Traminer Aromatico
NEW ZEALAND
  South Island Gewürztraminer
USA   Gewürztraminer

MEDIUM

AUSTRALIA   Gewürztraminer or Traminer
AUSTRIA   Gewürztraminer Spätlese
GERMANY   Gewürztraminer Spätlese
HUNGARY   Tramini
SOUTH AFRICA Gewürztraminer
USA
  California   Gewürztraminer
CROATIA   Traminac or Traminer Aromatico

SWEET

AUSTRALIA   Gewürztraminer Late Harvest
AUSTRIA & GERMANY
(in order of sweetness)
           Gewürztraminer Auslese, Gewürztraminer Beerenauslese, Gewürztraminer Trockenbeerenauslese
NEW ZEALAND Gewürztraminer Late Harvest
SOUTH AFRICA Gewürztraminer Late Harvest
USA
California   Gewürztraminer Late Harvest

PLAYING THE GAME

The Spice Of Life

Gewürztraminer is the most recognisable of white grapes because of its heady scent and pronounced spicy flavour. As a result, it is one of the few wines that will make an excellent partner for strong foods such as smoked fish, crabmeat or mature cheeses, as well as Indian, Chinese and Thai cuisine.

Game One
Dry

Gewürztraminer is not always over the top in its flavour and style. If you enjoy the grape but wish it was less overpowering, Italy provides the answer. So, try a Gewürztraminer from its native home in the Alto-Adige against a typical Alsace wine.

Heady Fragrance

Less Heady Fragrance

France
Alsace

Italy
Alto-Adige, Traminer Aromatico

A–B   — 2 to 3 years

Game Two
Medium

If you prefer a medium dry style, the warmer climates of southern Germany and eastern Europe provide the answer.

Germany
Pfalz, Kabinett

Vojvodina
Fruska Gora, Traminac

A–C   — 2 to 3 years

WHAT'S ON THE SHELVES

DRY

COUNTRY	COMMENTS		
ITALY **Trentino Alto-Adige**	Less aromatic and heady, so ideal if you like the grape but want a less powerful wine. ⊩▬▬ 1 to 5 years	**91, 90**	**A–B**

NEW ZEALAND
South Island
  Canterbury
  Marlborough
  Otago
	The most Alsace-like outside France. Excellent varietal character.
	⊩▬▬ 1 to 2 years
		91, 90	**B**

AUSTRIA **Burgenland** **Styria**	Dry wines with good alcohol levels. Full, spicy and flowery. ⊩▬▬ Young	**91, 90** **89**	**B**
FRANCE **Alsace**	The world's finest Gewürztraminers. Dry, quite high in alcohol. The best have the appellation 'Alsace Grand Cru'. 'Vendange Tardive' in good years are the most concentrated of dry Alsace wines and higher in alcohol. Spicy, intense flavours of lychees and mangoes with heady aromas. ⊩▬▬ 2 years. Grand Cru and Vendange. Tardive wines 4 to 10 years or more	**90, 89** **88, 86** **85, 83**	**A–D**
USA **Oregon**	A cool area with great potential. Alsace-style dry wines. ⊩▬▬ 2 to 6 years	**90, 89**	**B–C**

MEDIUM

GEWÜRZTRAMINER – WORLDWIDE & ALSACE

COUNTRY	COMMENTS		
AUSTRALIA **South Australia**	The best, from Eden Valley have typical characteristics of lychees and mangoes. 2 to 6 years	**90, 89** **87**	**B**
AUSTRIA **Burgenland** **Styria**	Medium dry to medium sweet wines will be labelled 'Spätlese'. Fuller than dry wines but can lack elegance. 2 to 6 years	**91, 90** **89, 88** **87**	**B–C**
FRANCE **Alsace**	Medium dry 'Vendange Tardive' made in exceptional years. Full, complex wines with strong varietal character, intense spiciness. 5 to 10 years and more	**90, 89** **88, 86** **85, 83** **81**	**C–D**
GERMANY **Baden** **Pfalz**	Lack acidity and tend to coarseness. Medium sweet are called 'Spätlese'. Off dry to medium dry. From 2 years, but wines become flat after 5	**90, 89** **88**	**B**
EASTERN EUROPE	The best come from Croatia and Slovenia. Medium dry to sweet with obvious varietal characteristics. 1 to 3 years	✗	**A**
NEW ZEALAND **North Island** **Gisborne**	Off-dry to medium dry, elegant with Alsace character but some residual sugar. 2 to 6 years	**90, 89** **88**	**B**
SOUTH AFRICA **Paarl** **Stellenbosch**	Spicy, floral. 2 to 5 years	**91, 90** **89**	**B–C**

COUNTRY	COMMENTS		
USA **California** Mendocino Napa Valley Sonoma	Off-dry with excellent varietal character. Pronounced smell and taste of lychees. From 2 to 6 years	90, 87 86	B–C

SWEET

COUNTRY	COMMENTS		
AUSTRIA **Burgenland**	Excellent, luscious and honeyed but lacking acidity. Within 5 to 7 years	91, 90 89, 88 87	B
FRANCE **Alsace**	'Sélection de grains nobles' only made in greatest years. Heady, powerful, with concentrated flavours. 4 to 10 years	90, 89 86, 85 83	D
GERMANY **Baden** **Pfalz**	Lack depth and complex tastes of Alsace. Low in acidity. From 4 to 6 years	90, 89 88	B
NEW ZEALAND **North Island**	Beautifully balanced 'Late Harvest' wines with good acidity and strong varietal character. 3 to 8 years	90, 89 88, 87 86, 85	B
SOUTH AFRICA **Paarl** **Stellenbosch**	Rare, rich honeyed 'noble rot' dessert wines – full, spicy and complex. Quite low in acidity. 5 to 10 years	91, 90 89, 88 87, 86 85	C
USA **California**	A few rich 'Late Harvest' dessert wines. Strong smell and taste of lychees. Less elegant than Alsace. 3 to 8 years	90, 87 86, 85	C

RELIABLE PRODUCERS & SHIPPERS

AUSTRALIA
Berri Estates, De Bortoli, Delatite, Forest Hill, McWilliams, Mildara, Orlando, Penfolds, Rosemount, Stanley Wine Co, Tisdall, Wyndham Estate

AUSTRIA
Sepp Hold

FRANCE
Alsace: Caves des Vignerons de Turckheim, Cooperative d'Eguisheim, Domaine Ostertag, Dopff au Moulin, Dopff et Irion, Gustave Lorentz, Hugel, Jean Preiss-Zimmer, Kuentz-Bas, Leon Beyer, Muré, Rolly Gassmann, Schlumberger, Theo Faller, Trimbach, Willy Gisselbrecht,

GERMANY
Badischer Zentralkellerei

ITALY
Anton von Elzenbaum, Hofstatter, Maso Foradore, Tiefenbrunner, Trattmanhof

NEW ZEALAND
Coopers Creek, Martinborough, Matawhero, Matua Valley, Morton Estate, Villa Maria, Weingut Seifried

SLOVENIA
Kutjevo Winery, Vitkovich

SOUTH AFRICA
Boschendal, Delheim, Fleur du Cap, Nederberg, Simonsig

USA
California: Adler Fells, Alexander Valley Vineyards, Ch St Jean, Firestone, Gundlach-Bundschu, Joseph Phelps, Mark West, Rutherford Hill, Wente Bros
Oregon: Elk Cove Vineyards, Kiona, Sokol Blosser, Tualatin
Washington State: Ch Ste Michelle, Staton Hills, Stewart Vineyards

CHARDONNAY
WORLDWIDE

FAMOUS REGION: BURGUNDY, FRANCE

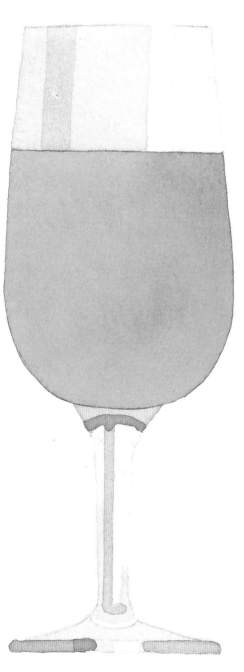

CHARDONNAY – WORLDWIDE

KNOW YOUR GRAPE

Chardonnay is the white grape which produces the world's best-known and most fashionable dry white wine.

Today, at least 12 countries, incorporating over 50 major wine regions, make top quality Chardonnays, many at very affordable prices.

Chardonnay's greatest attribute is that it is an easy-going grape which grows almost anywhere – from the coolest climates of northern France to the hottest in the Central Valley, of California – and seldom disappoints.

FLAVOURS

(CRISP APPLES) (BUTTER) (LEMONS) (FRUIT SALAD)

Chardonnay does not have an instantly recognisable flavour. Flavours range from crisp apples in cool climates such as Chablis, northern France, to fruit salad in New Zealand, lemons in Australia and a veritable cocktail in Côte d'Or, the premier region of Burgundy. Acidity in Chardonnay is most noticeable in cool climates such as Chablis, France, where the grapes are seldom as ripe as in, say, Australia or California.

STYLE

Always DRY

LIGHT　　**MEDIUM**　　**FULL**

✔　　✔　　✔

Depending on the ripeness of the grapes, wines vary from light to full. Always dry, but very ripe grapes from warm climates give an impression of richness.

WHEN TO DRINK

The lightest and freshest are best from 6 months to 2 years. The finest wines are all oak-aged (except some Chablis), medium to full in style and need time to mature. Particularly those from Burgundy.

HOW MUCH WILL IT COST?

A–D

IS IT EVER BLENDED WITH OTHER GRAPES?

Most Chardonnays are unblended but the Australians in particular experiment with other varieties. The grape is sometimes blended with Sémillon to add acidity and the label always shows this.

IS IT OAK-AGED?

Chardonnay responds extremely well to oak-ageing, used for most of the best wines. Light, crisp wines are made in steel or glass-lined tanks. See WHATS ON THE SHELVES.

IS THE GRAPE NAME ON THE LABEL?

Nearly always, except in Burgundy.

KNOW YOUR STYLE

STYLOMETER

LIGHT

NEW ZEALAND	South Island	Christchurch
AUSTRALIA	Tasmania	
FRANCE	Burgundy	Chablis (basic/generic)
	Loire	Haut Poitou, Touraine
ITALY	Trentino Alto-Adige, Friuli-Venezia-Giulia	
NEW ZEALAND	South Island	Canterbury, Marlborough, Nelson

MEDIUM

USA	Oregon	Willamette and Umpqua Valleys
AUSTRALIA	Victoria	Yarra Valley
	South Australia	Coonawarra, McLaren Vale
FRANCE	Burgundy	Chablis (Premier or Grand Cru) Côte Chalonnaise, Mâconnais
	Ardèche, Vin de Pays d'Oc	
NEW ZEALAND	North Island	Hawke's Bay, Gisborne, Henderson
AUSTRALIA	South Australia	Clare, Adelaide Hills
SPAIN	Penedés	
CHILE	Maipo, Curico	
USA	Washington State	Yakima Valley
NEW ZEALAND	North Island	Henderson
USA	California	Mendocino, Monterey, Carneros, Sonoma, Southern Napa, Santa Barbara
BULGARIA	Preslav, Khan Krum	
SOUTH AFRICA	Paarl, Stellenbosch, Robertson, Overberg	

FULL

FRANCE	Burgundy	Côte d'Or
USA	California	Northern Napa
AUSTRALIA	New South Wales	Hunter Valley, Riverina
	Western Australia	Swan Valley
	South Australia	Barossa Valley

MAKE THE GRAPE CONNECTION

LABELLED BY GRAPE

AUSTRALIA
BULGARIA
CHILE
FRANCE only in Haut Poitou
  Ardèche
  Languedoc-Roussillon (labelled Vin de Pays d'Oc)
  Touraine
  Some inexpensive white Burgundies
ITALY
NEW ZEALAND
SOUTH AFRICA
SPAIN
USA
  California
  New York (Finger Lakes and Long Island)
  Oregon
  Washington State

LABELLED BY REGION

BURGUNDY
Côte d'Or
  Auxey-Duresses
  Beaune
  Chassagne-Montrachet
  Corton-Charlemagne
  Meursault
  Monthélie
  Puligny-Montrachet
  St Aubin
  St Romain
Côte Chalonnaise
  Montagny
  Rully
Mâconnais
  Mâcon Blanc
  Mâcon-Clessé
  Mâcon-Lugny
  Mâcon-Prissé
  Mâcon Villages
  Mâcon-Viré
  Pouilly-Fuissé
  Pouilly-Loché
  Pouilly-Vincelles

PLAYING THE GAME

Lawrence

You will find more Chardonnays on the shelves from more countries of the world than any other white grape variety. However, although always dry, there is a good choice of lighter styles and the up-front, full taste so widely available from Australia. WHAT'S ON THE SHELVES (p.73) gives you a good selection but here are some ideas as a starter:

Game One
Chardonnay

Light

Chablis
(not Premier or Grand Cru)
Rhône Valley, France

or

Haut Poitou
Loire, France

or

Italy
Trentino Alto-Adige

Medium

Ardèche
France

or

Bulgaria
Khan Krum

or

Chile
Maipo Valley

𝒱

A–B ⌇⌇⌇⌇ France 3 years, Chile 2

Game Two
Chardonnay

Chardonnay responds particularly well to oak-ageing, giving the wines a complexity and depth of flavour that no other process achieves. The taste of oak is not everyone's choice, so to discover which wine you or your guests prefer, you could compare...

Unoaked

Chablis

or

Haut Poitou
Loire, France

Oaked

Australia
Hunter or Barossa Valley
(The label will tell you if the
wine is oak-aged)

or

for a lighter oak style try
New Zealand, North Island

√

A–B ⬕⬕▬▬ 3 years from France; 2 years from Australia

Game Three
Around the World

With so many Chardonnays to choose from, you could stage a fascinating tasting for a party or group of friends when the costs could be shared. Try a "1st XI" of different Chardonnays and see which country or region gets most votes, but ensure that all the labels are masked. A suggested line-up...

AUSTRALIA, Yarra Valley
AUSTRALIA, Hunter Valley
BULGARIA
CHILE
FRANCE, Chablis Premier Cru
FRANCE, Côte d'Or
FRANCE, Vin de Pays d'Oc
ITALY
NEW ZEALAND, North Island
USA, Napa Valley
USA, Oregon

⬕⬕▬▬ Spread the wines amongst all price bands, arranging them in any order *(see RELIABLE PRODUCERS & SHIPPERS P.76)*. Will you find the more expensive wines good value for money?

WHAT'S ON THE SHELVES

LIGHT

COUNTRY	COMMENTS		
AUSTRALIA			
Tasmania	One of Australia's coolest climates. Steely, Chablis-like wines with good acidity; crisp apples.	**91, 90**	**B**
	┃━ Young and fresh		
FRANCE			
Burgundy			
Chablis (basic/ generic wines)	See CHARDONNAY – WHITE BURGUNDY *(p.77)*.		
Loire	The cooperative at Neuville-de-Poitou produces	**91, 90**	**A**
Haut Poitou	very good value French Chardonnay.	**89**	
Touraine	Attractive fruity wine, with good acidity but softer and less distinctive than Chablis.		
	┃━ Young and fresh		
ITALY			
Friuli-Venezia-Giulia	Comparatively new in this region. More depth than those from Alto-Adige but with usually less oak-ageing.	**91, 90**	**B**
	┃━ Young and fresh		
Trentino Alto-Adige	The Italians usually use tanks, but oak-ageing	**91, 90**	**A**
	is on the increase. Light, buttery, grassy	**89**	
	flavours. Fresh Chablis-like with good acidity. Sometimes a slight prickle of carbon dioxide.		
	┃━ Young and fresh		
NEW ZEALAND			
South Island	The lightest of New Zealand Chardonnays.	**91, 90**	**B**
Canterbury	Nearly always matured in oak. Rich, buttery	**89, 88**	
Marlborough	flavours but more acidity and elegance	**87**	
Nelson	than North Island.		
	┃━ After 2 years. Most expensive will improve up to 5 or 6 years		

MEDIUM

COUNTRY	COMMENTS		
AUSTRALIA			
South Australia	Coolest of Australia's vineyards, so wines	91, 90	B–C
Adelaide Hills, Clare	are not as heavy and full-bodied as those	88, 87	
Coonawarra	from NSW or Barossa Valley. Characteristic	86	
McClaren Vale	golden colour, with smell of tropical fruit,		
Victoria	lychees, pineapples or maybe bananas.		
Yarra Valley	Lemony tang, fair acidity, rounded buttery		
Western Australia	flavour from oak-ageing.		
Margaret River	Less expensive, young and fresh. More		
Mount Barker	expensive from 3 to 6 years		
BULGARIA			
Khan Krum	Honest, sound wines at remarkable prices.	90, 89	A
Preslav	Fresh, with good acidity but lack real buttery, fruit flavour. Better wines are oak-aged giving a rather dry finish.		
	Young and fresh		
CHILE			
Central Valley	Improving with every vintage and beginning	91, 90	A
Curico	to master the varietal flavours of Chardonnay.	88	
Maipo	Oak-aged. Traditional buttery overtones.		
	2 to 6 years		
FRANCE			
Burgundy			
Chablis	Premier and Grand Cru. See CHARDONNAY – WHITE BURGUNDY (p.77).		
Côte Chalonnaise	See CHARDONNAY – WHITE BURGUNDY (p.77).		
Mâconnais	See CHARDONNAY – WHITE BURGUNDY (p.77).		
Ardèche	Soft, fresh fruit flavours, Mâcon style.	90, 89	B
	Young and fresh		
Vin de Pays d'Oc	Tropical fruit flavours.	90, 89	B
	2 to 4 years		
NEW ZEALAND			
North Island	Well-made, complex wines nearly always	91, 90	B
Gisborne	oak-aged. Rich, buttery flavours with	89, 88	
Hawkes Bay	balancing acidity.	87	
Henderson	3 years onwards		

COUNTRY	COMMENTS		

SOUTH AFRICA
  Overberg
  Paarl
  Robertson
  Stellenbosch
	Very successful and easier to find, now
	South Africa has come in from the cold.
	Usually big, oak-aged, with citrus, peaches
	and almond flavours.
	▐◄▬ 2 to 8 years
		91, 90
		89
			B–C

SPAIN Penedés	Comparatively new to Spain. Excellent value. Good varietal character, oak-aged. ▐◄▬ 2 to 5 years	91, 90 89, 88	B

USA
  Washington State
    Yakima Valley
	Warmer than Oregon, cooler than much
	of California. Usually soft, muted buttery taste.
	▐◄▬ 2 to 3 years, up to 6
		90, 89
		88
			B

California
  Carneros
  Mendocino
  Monterey
  Santa Barbara
  Sonoma
  Southern Napa
	Larger than life, but trend is toward more
	elegant, less powerful wines, particularly in
	cooler areas. Cheaper wines spoilt by an
	excess of oak. The best achieve Burgundian
	elegance with acidity and delicately toasted
	nutty and buttery flavours. Golden colour,
	pronounced bouquet.
	▐◄▬ 3 to 8 years
		90, 89
		88, 86
			A–B

Oregon
  Umpqua Valley
  Willamette Valley
	Chablis-like. High priced. Crisp, appley
	and fresh.
	▐◄▬ Young and fresh
		90, 89
		88
			C

FULL

AUSTRALIA
  New South Wales
    Hunter Valley
  South Australia
    Barossa Valley
  Western Australia
    Swan River
	Real impact of flavour but lack elegance of
	cooler climate wines. Big, powerful, full
	flavoured. Lemony with flavours of exotic
	fruit, pineapples and mangoes, as well as
	buttery fruit from oak-ageing.
	▐◄▬ 3 years plus
		91, 90
		88, 86
			A–C

FRANCE
  Burgundy
    Côte d'Or
	See CHARDONNAY – WHITE BURGUNDY (p.77).		

USA
  California
    Northern
    Napa Valley
	Full-bodied with alcoholic strength of 13° or
	more. Rich, buttery flavours, green-gold colour.
	▐◄▬ Sometimes lack acidity, so drink 3 to
	6 years – the less expensive become
	tired after 4 years
		90, 89
		88, 87
		86, 85
			B–C

RELIABLE PRODUCERS & SHIPPERS

LIGHT

FRANCE
Anjou/Touraine: Vignerons de Oisly et Thesée
Chablis: Bacheroy-Josselin, Cave Cooperative La Chablisienne, Francois Raveneau, Jean Durup, Jean-Marc Brocard, Joseph Drouhin, Louis Michel, Philippe Testut, William Fèvre
Haut Poitou: Cave Cooperative de Haut Poitou

ITALY
Trentino Alto-Adige: Alois Lageder, J Tiefenbrunner, Santa Margherita, Winzergenossenschaft Südtirol

NEW ZEALAND
Giesen, Montana, St Helena

USA
Oregon: Alpine Vineyards, Eyrie Vineyards, Knudsen Erath, Tualatin.

MEDIUM

AUSTRALIA
Bannockburn, Brown Brothers (Whitlands Vineyard), Forest Hill, Jeffrey Grosset, Leeuwin Estate, Orlando, Petaluma, Rouge Homme, Tisdall, Tyrrells.

BULGARIA
Khan Krum

CHILE
Concha y Toro, Cousino Macul, Errazuriz Panquehue, Santa Marta, Santa Rita, Torres

FRANCE
Ardèche: Louis Latour
Côte de Beaune, Côte Chalonnaise, Mâconnais: see CHARDONNAY – WHITE BURGUNDY *(starts opposite)*

NEW ZEALAND
Babich, Cloudy Bay, Cooks, Coopers Creek, Delegats, Hunters, Kumeu River, Martinborough, Matua Valley, Montana, Morton Estate, Nobilo, Selaks, Stoneleigh Vineyard, Te Mata, Vidal, Villa Maria

SOUTH AFRICA
Boschendal, De Wetshof, Hamilton-Russel, Nederberg, Overgaauw, Rustenberg, Simonsig

SPAIN
Raimat, Torres

USA
California: Acacia, Alexander Valley Vineyards, Beaulieu, Berringer, Chalone, Christian Brothers, Clos du Bois, Clos du Val, Cuvaison, Fetzer, Frog's Leap, Glen Ellen, Heitz, Iron Horse, Jekel, Joseph Phelps, Matanzas Creek, Mayacamas, Mondavi, Monterey Vineyard, Monticello, Newton, Rutherford Hill, Saintsbury, Simi, Sonoma-Cutrer, Stag's Leap Wine Cellars, Swanson Vineyards, Trefethen, 'ZD'

FULL

AUSTRALIA
Allandale, Berri Estates, Bowen Estate, Brown Brothers, Geoff Merrill, Hardy's, Hill-Smith Estate, Houghton, Hungerford Hill, Lake's Folly, Lindemans, Mildara, Montrose, Orlando Penfolds, Peterson, Rosemount Estate, Rothbury Estate, Saltram, Taltarni, Wolf Blass

USA
California: Firestone, Inglenook, Mount St Helena, Sterling Vineyards, Wente Brothers

CHARDONNAY
WHITE BURGUNDY

(BOURGOGNE BLANC)

KNOW YOUR GRAPE

To get an overall view of Chardonnay, you should read the preceding guide first and see the different tastes and styles around the world. This guide deals solely with the classic region for Chardonnay; Burgundy. Here the grape reaches pinnacles of subtlety and complexity unrivalled anywhere else. Burgundy produces the world's most fabled and highly prized dry white wines.

White Burgundy is made exclusively from Chardonnay except for Bourgogne Aligoté. A less expensive, sharper grape whose name always appears on the label.

The world famous Chardonnays include such household names as Chablis, Mâcon, Meursault, Montrachet and Pouilly Fuissé, but the grape name rarely appears on the label. Surprisingly for a variety that grows in most climates, Chardonnay represents a mere 20% of Burgundy's total production. The rest comprises the red Burgundies from the Pinot Noir grape and Beaujolais wines from the Gamay grape.

FLAVOURS

Wines have an unmatched elegance and a marvellous range of flavours which vary from region to region and even village to village. See WHAT'S ON THE SHELVES (p.85)

STYLE

Always DRY

LIGHT	MEDIUM	FULL
✔	✔	✔

WHEN TO DRINK

Drink Bourgogne Blanc, the cheapest Chablis and Mâcon Blanc young and fresh. Village wines from 3 to 10 years or 15 years for the very best, dependent on the vintage.

IS IT OAK-AGED?

In Burgundy, oak-ageing is common and used with instinctive subtlety, so it is rare for white Burgundy to be over-oaked. In Chablis however, although traditional winemakers use oak, others claim it destroys the characteristic steely, mineral flavour. See pro-oak or tank producers (p.204).

HOW MUCH WILL IT COST?

A–D

Regional wines are likely to be in **A**, the bulk of village wines in **B–C**. The really great wines in **D**.

IS IT EVER BLENDED WITH OTHER GRAPES?

No. Blending is not allowed by law.

IS THE GRAPE NAME ON THE LABEL?

No. Very rarely on some basic regional wines.

KNOW YOUR STYLE

Chardonnay grows on most soils but particularly loves limestone, hence its affinity with certain parts of Burgundy, where the wines cover the taste spectrum, varying from region to region and village to village. As Burgundy's vineyards are spread over some 160 miles from north to south, the weather plays an important role in the style of the wines.

THE FOUR WHITE BURGUNDY REGIONS

CHABLIS

Cold, sometimes very bitter winters, prone to spring frost.

FLAVOURS

Dry, steely, crisp apples, with marked acidity in basic wines, less noticeable in Premier and Grand Cru wines.

STYLE

LIGHT	MEDIUM	FULL
✔	✘	✔
Basic wines		Premier & Grand Cru

COTE D'OR

Côte de Beaune & Côte de Nuits

The weather is less severe than in Chablis. The Côte (hill) protects the vineyards from westerly winds and provides an ideal south-easterly exposure to the sun.

FLAVOURS

Acidity less noticeable than Chablis. See WHAT'S ON THE SHELVES *(p.85)*.

STYLE

LIGHT	MEDIUM	FULL
✘	✔	✔

COTE CHALONNAISE

A hilly, slightly cooler region than the Côte d'Or, so the wines are less full.

FLAVOURS

Spicy, honey, almonds, with noticeable acidity.

STYLE

LIGHT	MEDIUM	FULL
✘	✔	✘

MACONNAIS

The largest white wine region. Very cold winters but hot summers which produce ripe grapes. The best value Burgundies.

FLAVOURS

Flowery, fresh fruit, with less noticeable acidity than Côte Chalonnaise or Chablis.

STYLE

LIGHT	MEDIUM	FULL
✘	✔	✘

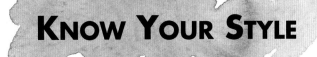

KNOW YOUR STYLE

STYLOMETER

LIGHT

Bourgogne Blanc
Chablis   Petit Chablis, Chablis

MEDIUM

Beaujolais
Mâconnais   Mâcon
Côte Chalonnaise Givry, Montagny, Rully
Côte de Beaune   St Romain, St Aubin, Beaune,
                     Pernand-Vergelesses
Mâconnais   Mâcon Villages, Mâcon-Clessé, Mâcon-Lugny,
                     Mâcon-Prissé, Mâcon-Viré, Pouilly-Loché,
                     Pouilly-Vinzelles, Pouilly-Fuissé, St Veran

FULL

Côte de Beaune   Aloxe-Corton, Auxey-Duresses, Meursault,
                     Chassagne-Montrachet, Puligny-Montrachet
Chablis   Chablis Premier Cru
Côte de Beaune   Meursault Premier Cru, Chassagne-Montrachet,
                     Puligny-Montrachet Premier Cru
Chablis   Chablis Grand Cru
Côte de Beaune   Corton-Charlemagne, Grands Crus in
                     Puligny-Montrachet

MAKE THE GRAPE CONNECTION

APPELLATION CONTROLEE

All wines with the name 'Bourgogne' qualify for an 'Appellation Contrôlée', a controlled name. The AC, as it is known, relates to a specific piece of land and is a guarantee of origin only. There are five levels of AC in Burgundy. The smaller the named area, the finer and more expensive the wine.

GRANDS CRUS

PREMIERS CRUS
Almost top rank.

VILLAGES within regions
Wines produced in specific villages. Best quality after Premiers and Grands Crus.

REGIONS within Burgundy
Sound everyday wines with broad characteristics of the region.

BURGUNDY (Bourgogne) – the whole area
The basic AC is usually dull and overpriced.

CHARDONNAY – WHITE BURGUNDY

The names on the label will tell you whether the wine comes from anywhere in Burgundy, or from a specific region, a named village or even a vineyard within a village.

REGION

BURGUNDY
i.e. the whole area

REGIONS within Burgundy

VILLAGES within the regions
Wines produced in specified villages. This level provides the best quality wines before the pricey super-stars of Premier and Grand Cru. Labels may include a vineyard name but, unless a Premier or Grand Cru *(see below)*, it does not necessarily mean the wine is any better than the straight village wines.

PREMIER CRU vineyards
In Chablis and within some of the villages of the Côte d'Or, there are two top levels of AC – the Premiers and Grands Crus – 'Cru' meaning growth. Illogically, Premier means first but is outranked by Grand! These wines are the *crème de la crème*. Listed here are some of the better-known.

GRAND CRU vineyards
(Each with its own AC in Côte d'Or)

LABELLED AS

**Bourgogne,
Bourgogne Grand Ordinaire**

Chablis, Côte d'Or (Côte de Nuits and Côte de Beaune), Côte Chalonnaise, Mâconnais and Beaujolais

Côte Chalonnaise: Givry, Montagny, Rully
Côte de Beaune: Aloxe-Corton, Auxey-Duresses, Beaune, Chassagne-Montrachet, Meursault, Puligny-Montrachet, Pernand-Vergelesses, St Aubin, St Romain
Mâconnais: Mâcon-Clessé, Mâcon-Lugny, Mâcon-Prissé, Mâcon-Viré, Mâcon Villages, Pouilly-Fuissé, Pouilly-Loché, Pouilly-Vinzelles St Veran

Chablis
Beauroy Montmains, Côte de Léchet, Fourchaume, Les Fourneaux, Mélinots, Montée de Tonnerre, Monts de Milieus, Vaillons, Vaudevey, Vosgros, Vaucoupin
Côte de Beaune
Chassagne-Montrachet – Clos-St Jean, Grandes Ruchottes, La Maltroie, La Romanée, Les Brussonnes, Les Champs Gain, Les Chenevottes, Les Macherelles, Les Vergers, Morgeots
Meursault – Les Bouchères, Les Charmes, Les Genevrières, Les Gouttes d'Or, Les Perrières
Puligny-Montrachet – Clavaillon, La Garenne, Le Cailleret, Les Champs Canet, Les Combottes, Les Folatières, Les Pucelles,

Chablis
Blanchot, Bougros, Grenouilles, La Moutonne, Les Clos, Les Preuses, Valmur, Vaudésir
Côte de Beaune
Aloxe-Corton – Corton-Charlemagne
Puligny-Montrachet – Bâtard-Montrachet, Bienvenues-Bâtard-Montrachet, Chevalier-Montrachet, Le Montrachet

PLAYING THE GAME

As Burgundy's vineyards are spread over such a wide area there is a marked difference in style, taste and price. The following comparisons illustrate the distinction between the four main areas. You may, of course, compare all four together. With Burgundy, the name of the grower or shipper is very important (see p.90).

Game One
Chardonnay Regions

Chablis (not Premier or Grand Cru) or **Côte de Beaune Villages** Côte de Beaune	**Rully** Côte Chalonnaise or **Mâcon Blanc** Mâconnais

B-C 3 years

Game Two
Villages

The following comparisons are designed to show the most marked differences. Ranging from the steely character of Chablis to the almost Côte de Beaune style of the Côte Chalonnaise, or the stylishness of the Côte de Beaune against the much rounder style of the Mâconnais.

Chablis Premier Cru
or
St Aubin or **St Romain**
Côte de Beaune

C

Montagny
Côte Chalonnaise
or
Mâcon-Lugny/Mâcon Prissé
Mâconnais

or

Chablis Grand Cru
or
Puligny-Montrachet
Côte de Beaune

D 3 years

Montagny
Côte Chalonnaise
or
Pouilly Fuissé
Mâconnais

CHARDONNAY – WHITE BURGUNDY

Game Three
Millionaire's Row

A fascinating (though expensive) tasting is to compare the world's three greatest Chardonnay vineyards and so discover their subtleties and complexities. It is important that the wines you choose should all be of the same quality. All straightforward village wines, or all Premier Crus.

Puligny-Montrachet ∨ **Chassagne-Montrachet** ∨ **Meursault**

D ⊫— 1986

Game Four
Burgundy against 'The World'

Chardonnay is currently the world's most popular white wine, but which country produces the style you prefer? If Burgundy is already your love, it is unlikely that you will change your views; but have you compared some of the wines from the newer, cooler regions in Australia, New Zealand and North America? Or, if you are a devotee of these countries, have you ever compared them against Burgundy? At the top level, they compete very well with the best from Burgundy.

Burgundy

Meursault
Côte de Beaune
or
Chassagne Montrachet
Côte de Beaune
or
Puligny-Montrachet
Côte de Beaune

∨

The World

Australia
South Australia, Western Australia
or Victoria
or
USA
California or Oregon
or Washington State

B–D ⊫— 3 years from France, 2 years from Australia and USA

The wines from Australia and the USA may taste fuller because of the concentration of fruit in the riper grapes. Try and select those that are 12° to 13° for a fair comparison.

WHAT'S ON THE SHELVES

Because the weather is so changeable in Burgundy, the vintage is especially important. We give vintage guidance separately and in detail on p.88.

LIGHT

COUNTRY	COMMENTS	
BOURGOGNE BLANC from anywhere in region	Basic white Burgundy, high in acidity except in best years. Plain Mâcon is better value, usually with more fruit. Young and fresh	**A–B**
PETIT CHABLIS Chablis	Often too sharp and lacking in fruit. Young – if at all!	**B**
CHABLIS Chablis	Herby, aromatic smell, noticeable acidity and steely flavour with taste of green apples. Young and fresh	**B–C**

MEDIUM

COUNTRY	COMMENTS	
BEAUJOLAIS	Small production, but increasingly seen. Fresh, peach fruit. 2 to 4 years	**B**
BEAUNE Côte de Beaune	Elegant wines with flowery taste and smell. 2 to 4 years	**C**

COUNTRY	COMMENTS	
GIVRY **Côte Chalonnaise**	Small production. Delicious spicy flavour. 2 to 4 years	**B**
MACON **Mâconnais**	Basic Mâcon, probably made in co-operative and none the worse for that. Usually very good value. Fresh, flowery and fruity. 1 to 2 years	**B**
MACON VILLAGES **Mâconnais**	Forty-two villages can use this AC. Best known are Mâcon-Clessé, Mâcon-Lugny, Mâcon-Prissé and Mâcon-Viré. Usually made in tanks. Dry with flowery smell and fresh fruit flavours. Clessé wines are particularly elegant. Young, 2 to 3 years	**B–C**
MONTAGNY **Côte Chalonnaise**	Driest of Chalonnaise white wines, quite full, with refreshing crispness and honey and almond flavours. 2 to 4 years	**B**
PERNAND-VERGELESSES **Côte de Beaune**	Round, fruity and well-balanced wines of style and character. 2 to 5 years	**C**
POUILLY-FUISSE **Mâconnais**	Best known and most expensive of Mâconnais wines. Best are oak-aged with full, buttery flavour. Very best are similar to Côte d'Or wines. Pouilly-Loché, Pouilly-Vinzelles and St Veran. 2 to 4 years, up to 6 for Pouilly Fuissé	**B–D**
RULLY **Côte Chalonnaise**	Light, spicy and herby. 2 to 4 years	**B**
ST AUBIN **Côte de Beaune**	Quite full with taste of hazelnuts and a toasty flavour. Similar style to, but better value than plain Puligny-Montrachet. 2 to 5 years	**C–D**
ST ROMAIN **Côte de Beaune**	Good, sound fresh wines. 2 to 4 years	**C**

FULL

COUNTRY	COMMENTS	
AUXEY-DURESSES **Côte de Beaune**	Biscuity flavour and flowery smell. 2 to 4 years except best vintages	C
CHABLIS PREMIERS **& GRANDS CRUS** **Chablis**	Although always dry, these are fullest Chablis wines with most fruit and flavour. From 3 years, but best will continue to improve up to 6 or 7	D
CHASSAGNE- **MONTRACHET** **Côte de Beaune**	The real class is in the Premiers Crus. Honey and almonds with almost smoky smell. 3 to 10 years	D
CORTON- **CHARLEMAGNE** **Côte de Beaune**	One of the great and most expensive white Burgundies. Full, buttery with taste of almonds. Big, honeyed smell and peppery undertones. Wines to keep from 5 to 10 years	D
MEURSAULT **Côte de Beaune**	World famous. White Burgundy at its best. Big and rich with flavour of peaches and honey. Strong, nutty, spicy smelling wines. Keep up to 4 years before drinking, the best will keep up to 10	D
PULIGNY- **MONTRACHET** **Côte de Beaune**	Generally better than Chassagne-Montrachet. Le Montrachet, the most famous, has some of the greatest Premiers and Grands Crus. Honey and almonds with finesse and elegance. All qualities a minimum of 4 years old, 10 or more for best from great vintages	D

CHARDONNAY – WHITE BURGUNDY

VINTAGES

CHABLIS

1983
Excellent, well balanced wines with ripe fruit giving a softer edge. Even the best Premiers and Grands Crus are now showing signs of old age.

1984
Much better in Chablis than Côte d'Or. A classic year, with wines showing the typical steely character. Premiers and Grands Crus are at their best now.

1985
Untypical year. Full, soft wines more in the style of southern Burgundies. Drink now.

1986
Excellent, stylish Chablis vintage with very good acidity and flavour, but high prices. Good for drinking now but top wines will keep a few years yet.

1987
Another excellent year but a low crop and, therefore, expensive. In style, somewhere between '85 and '86.

1988
Yet another successful year. Good, ripe grapes and so less of the classic Chablis style. Wines have depth and are ready for drinking now, the best will improve for another year.

1989
Small, very fine vintage, with more fruit and softness than normal in Chablis. Basic wines can be drunk now but the best need time to develop.

1990
A much larger crop than anyone expected. The grapes were ripe and the acidity level quite low, so do not expect the crisp Chablis style in this year.

1991
A straightforward vintage of average quality. Good, solid wines which should mature well.

COTE D'OR, COTE CHALONNAISE & MACONNAIS

1982
Big, generous vintage, soft in character. Overproduction made many of the flavours a bit muted and most of the wines are either at their best or over the hill.

1983
Very patchy year dependent on when the grapes were picked. Those who picked early made beautiful, balanced wine. Those who picked late had to struggle with the problems that over-ripe grapes produce and wines are untypically high in alcohol.

1984
Disappointing year but wines are perfectly adequate, if a bit short of fruit. Drink now.

1985
Enormously rich year. Full wines balanced by good acidity without which they would have been 'blowsy'. This is a year for those who like Australian or Californian Chardonnays but with a little more elegance. No trouble about keeping them.

1986
Most classic and probably the best of Chardonnay vintages in Burgundy and one of the more expensive. Wines are very stylish with good acidity, generally elegant, ready for drinking now.

1987

Much better year for whites than reds. Sound, decent wines. Drink now but still overpriced.

1988

Not unlike '87 in style, but grapes were riper and wines have more depth and character. Lesser wines are drinkable now but most will benefit from another year or two in the bottle.

1989

A small but excellent vintage, not only in quality but, again, in price. The most successful wines have good balance of fruit and acidity but some suffer from over-ripe grapes and the problems they bring to vinification. The better wines need another year or so to develop but are unlikely to be very long lived.

1990

Opinions differ about the style of the 1990s, although all are agreed that the yield was far greater than expected. It is too early to know how the wines will develop but it is likely that they will be on the soft side and cheaper than recent vintages.

1991

Apart from a few problems with hail in the summer, the harvest is only just below the level of 1990 in quantity and average to good quality.

RELIABLE PRODUCERS AND SHIPPERS

CHABLIS
Growers who age in oak
Domaine Servin, Francois Raveneau, Jean-Marc Brocard, Jean-Paul Droin, Louis Pinson, Rene Dauvissat, William Fèvre
Growers who use stainless steel
Alain Geoffroy, Cave Cooperative la Chablisienne, Bernard Defaix, Jean Durup, Louis Michel, Robert Vocoret
Merchants
A Regnard, Bacheroy-Josselin, Joseph Drouhin, Labouré-Roi, Moreau, Simmonet-Febvre

COTE D'OR
Aloxe-Corton
Bonneau de Martray, Bouchard Père et Fils, Chartron et Trebuchet, Domaine de la Reine Pédauque, Jaffelin, J-F Coche-Dury, Joseph Drouhin, Louis Jadot, Moillard, Remoissenet, Michel Voarick, Olivier Leflaive
Auxey-Duresses
Bouchard Père et Fils, Domaine du Duc de Magenta, Domaine Leroy, Michel Prunier, Robert Ampeau,
Chassagne-Montrachet
Bernard Morey, Chartron et Trebuchet, Delagrange-Bachelet, Domaine Albert Morey, Domaine Jean-Noel Gagnard, Domaine Ramonet, Etienne Sauzet, Gagnard-Delagrange, Hubert Lamy, Joseph Drouhin, Labouré-Roi, Lequin-Roussot, Louis Carillon, Louis Jadot, Louis Latour, Moillard, Olivier Leflaive, Raoul Clerget, Remoissenet
Meursault
Antonin Guyon, Bouchard Père et Fils, Chartron et Trebuchet, Domaine de la Reine Pédauque, Domaine des Comtes Lafon, Domaine du Ch de Meursault, Francois Jobard, Guy Roulot, Jaffelin, Jean Germain, Jean Monnier et Fils, J-F Coche-Dury, Louis Jadot, Louis Latour, Maison Leroy, Michel Lafarge, Michelot-Buisson, Olivier Leflaive, Pierre Morey, Prosper Maufoux, Rene Monnier, Robert Ampeau, Ropiteau Frères

Puligny-Montrachet
Chartron et Trebuchet, Domaine de la Reine Pédauque, Domaine du Ch de Meursault, Domaine Gagnard-Delagrange, Domaine Leflaive, Etienne Sauzet, Jacques Prieur, Jean Germain, Joseph Drouhin, Louis Carillon et Fils, Louis Jadot, Lequin-Roussot, Maison Leroy, Olivier Leflaive, Prosper Maufoux, René Monnier, Raoul Clerget, Remoissenet, Robert Ampeau, Roux Père et Fils
St Aubin
Chartron et Trebuchet, Domaine de la Reine Pédauque, Henri Prudhon, Hubert Lamy, Jaffelin, Olivier Leflaive, Prosper Maufoux, Raoul Clerget, Roux Père et Fils
St Romain
Domaine du Ch de Puligny-Montrachet, Domaine René Thévenin-Monthélie, Jaffelin
Savigny-les Beaune, Beaune, Monthelie
Domaine du Ch de Meursault, Bouchard Père et Fils, Garaudet, Louis Jadot, Pierre Bitouzet, Simon Bize et Fils

COTE CHALONNAISE
Rully
Chartron et Trebuchet, Domaine de la Folie, Domaine de la Renarde, Jaffelin, Michel Juillot, Raoul Clerget, Ropiteau Frères
Montagny
B and J-M Delauhay, Caves des Vignerons de Buxy, Louis Latour, Michel Goubard

MACONNAIS
Cave Cooperative de Prissé, Cave de Viré, Cave des Vignerons de Buxy,
Mâcon Villages
Ch de la Greffière, Henri Lafarge, Jean Signoret, Jean Thevenet

SÉMILLON
AUSTRALIA & BORDEAUX

SÉMILLON – AUSTRALIA & BORDEAUX

KNOW YOUR GRAPE

Sémillon is a French grape and, like Chenin Blanc, very versatile. It produces both dry and very sweet white wines of world class, yet the name never appears on French labels and its importance goes unnoticed. Without Sémillon there would be very little white Bordeaux, certainly none of the great dessert wines of Sauternes and Barsac. Sémillon in France produces wines low in acidity but they are big and alcoholic. When dry they are rather pedestrian, when sweet they can become too cloying. So, for both dry and sweet wines, it is almost always blended with Sauvignon Blanc to gain freshness and acidity.

In Australia, Sémillon is recognised as an important variety in its own right. The wines are mainly dry, although exciting sweet wines are now made.

FLAVOURS

BUTTERY HONEY CITRUS FIGS

Hint of citrus, more noticeable in Australia, and an impression of sweetness even when dry. Sometimes a flavour of figs. Buttery when aged in oak. The sweeter wines are honeyed and voluptuous, particularly when affected by 'noble rot' – see WINEMAKING (p.204). Acidity lower than other white varieties.

STYLE

DRY	MEDIUM	SWEET
✔	✘	✔

Medium to full-bodied. High in alcohol. Golden colour, very deep when mature, with orange and mahogany tints.

IS IT OAK-AGED?

Sémillon responds well to oak-ageing and most Australian and the best French wines are both fermented and matured in small oak barrels.

HOW MUCH WILL IT COST?

A–D

The great wines in both Australia and France are mainly in band **D**.

WHEN TO DRINK

When dry and blended with Sauvignon Blanc, drink French wines young and fresh. Only the very fine white Graves wines need 3 to 4 years before developing their full flavours. Sweet wines are a matter of personal taste but will be too cloying before 3 to 4 years and the best last for 10 years and more.

IS IT EVER BLENDED WITH OTHER GRAPES?

Invariably in Bordeaux, with Sauvignon Blanc. Increasingly in Australia where winegrowers are blending with other varieties to produce more complex flavours.

IS THE GRAPE NAME ON THE LABEL?

Yes, in Australia. Rarely in Bordeaux.

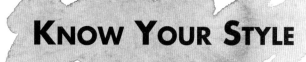

KNOW YOUR STYLE

Although Sémillon varies from dry to sweet both in France and Australia, the winemaker may produce either styles from the same vineyard or winery. This Stylometer gives a very general guide to the regional styles.

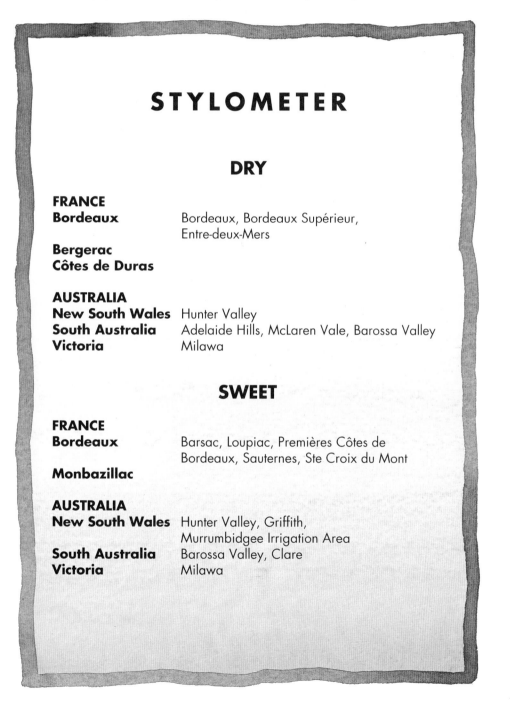

STYLOMETER

DRY

FRANCE
Bordeaux   Bordeaux, Bordeaux Supérieur, Entre-deux-Mers

Bergerac
Côtes de Duras

AUSTRALIA
New South Wales   Hunter Valley
South Australia   Adelaide Hills, McLaren Vale, Barossa Valley
Victoria   Milawa

SWEET

FRANCE
Bordeaux   Barsac, Loupiac, Premières Côtes de Bordeaux, Sauternes, Ste Croix du Mont

Monbazillac

AUSTRALIA
New South Wales   Hunter Valley, Griffith, Murrumbidgee Irrigation Area
South Australia   Barossa Valley, Clare
Victoria   Milawa

MAKE THE GRAPE CONNECTION

LABELLED BY GRAPE

DRY

AUSTRALIA
(If other grapes are blended in, the label says so)

LABELLED BY REGION

DRY

FRANCE
Bordeaux
  Entre-deux-Mers
  Graves
Bergerac
Côtes de Duras

SWEET

FRANCE
Bordeaux
  Premières Côtes de Bordeaux
  Barsac
  Loupiac
  Ste Croix du Mont
  Sauternes
Monbazillac

PLAYING THE GAME

Game One
Dry

100%

Sémillon, Australia
NSW or South Australia

Blended

 **Graves** or **Entre-deux-Mers**
Bordeaux, France

A–B 3 years from France, 2 years from Australia

Game Two
Sweet

100%

Sémillon, Australia
NSW, Victoria or South Australia

Blended

Sauternes or **Barsac**
Bordeaux, France

A–B 4 years from France, 3 years from Australia. Sweet wines become drier with age and after 4 years the sweetness becomes less overpowering

If you find the 100% sweet wine too cloying, this may be because the level of acidity is low. If so, next time try a sweet Chenin Blanc.

WHAT'S ON THE SHELVES

100% SÉMILLON – DRY

COUNTRY	COMMENTS		
AUSTRALIA			
Barossa Valley	High class, good value, under-rated. Pronounced lemony taste, full-bodied. 🍷~~~ 3 to 10 years or more	91, 90 89, 87 86	A–B
Hunter Valley	Great dry white wines. Toasty, buttery, nutty, full-bodied. 🍷~~~ 3 to 20+ years	91, 90 88, 87 86, 85 83	A–D
Victoria	Lemony flavour. Lighter than Hunter and Barossa wines. 🍷~~~ 3 to 8 years	90, 89 87, 86	A–B
FRANCE			
Bordeaux	Ch Rahoul (Graves) and very few others. Full-flavoured, elegant, dry. Rich and honeyed. 🍷~~~ 3 to 10 years	90, 88 87, 86	B–D

100% SÉMILLON – SWEET

COUNTRY	COMMENTS		
AUSTRALIA			

New South Wales
  Griffith
  Hunter Valley
  Murrumbidgee
	Luscious with apricot flavours.
	🍷~~~ 3 years, then as long as you have
	patience
		91, 90
		88, 87
		86, 85
			B
			(half
			bottle)

South Australia **Barossa Valley**	Lemony, rich without 'zip' and honey flavour of 'noble rot'. 🍷~~~ 3 to 10 years	84, 82	B

COUNTRY	COMMENTS		
FRANCE			
Bordeaux	Ch Doisy-Daëne (Sauternes) is one of the rare	**90, 89**	**D**
	unblended Sémillons. Rich and honeyed.	**88, 86**	
	▌◄═══ 4 to 10 years, more in best years	**85, 83, 81**	

BLENDED WITH SAUVIGNON BLANC – DRY

FRANCE			
Bergerac	Freshness and 'zing' from Sauvignon Blanc.	**90, 89**	**A–D**
Bordeaux	Only the best Graves are memorable	**88, 87**	
Entre-deux-Mers	making the rich, full wines, dry but honeyed.	**86, 83**	
Graves	▌◄═══ Young and fresh for inexpensive		
Côtes de Duras	wines. Fine Graves needs 3 years,		
	10 or more for the best		

BLENDED WITH SAUVIGNON BLANC – SWEET

FRANCE			
Bordeaux	Among the world's greatest dessert wines.	**90, 89**	**A–D**
Barsac	Luscious, honey-sweet with tastes of apricots	**88, 86**	
Loupiac	and peaches. High in alcohol.	**85, 83**	
Premières Côtes de	▌◄═══ The less expensive at 2 years, the		
Bordeaux	finest from 4 years to 20+ years		
Ste Croix-du Mont			
Sauternes			
Monbazillac			

BLENDED WITH CHARDONNAY – DRY

AUSTRALIA			
Hunter Valley	Chardonnay adds acidity. Overall taste and	**91, 90**	**A**
New South Wales	character similar to unblended Sémillon.		
South Australia	▌◄═══ Young and fresh		

SÉMILLON – AUSTRALIA & BORDEAUX

RELIABLE PRODUCERS & SHIPPERS

100%

DRY

AUSTRALIA
Hunter Valley, NSW
Allandale, Hungerford Hill, Lindemans, McWilliams, Rothbury Estate, Tyrrels, Wyndham Estate
South Australia
Geoff Merrill (McLaren Vale), Henschke (Adelaide Hills), Orlando (Barossa Valley), Penfolds (Barossa Valley), Rockford (Barossa Valley), Seppelt (Barossa Valley)
Victoria
Brown Brothers, Taltarni

FRANCE
Bordeaux
Ch Rahoul (Graves)

SWEET

AUSTRALIA
Griffith, NSW
De Bortoli
Murrumbidgee Irrigation Area, NSW
Lindemans, McWilliams, Orlando

FRANCE
Bordeaux
Ch Doisy-Daëne (Sauternes)

BLENDED

DRY

FRANCE
Bordeaux
Entre-deux-Mers – Ch Bonnet
Graves – Ch Cabannieux, Ch d'Archambeau, Ch La Tour Martillac, Ch Laville-Haut Brion, Ch Olivier, Ch Malartic Lagravière, Domaine de Chevalier, 'R de Rieussec', Vin sec du Ch Coutet,

SWEET

FRANCE
Bordeaux
Sauternes and Barsac – Ch Bastor-Lamontagne, Ch Broustet, Ch Cantegril, Ch Chartreuse, Ch Climens, Ch Coutet, Ch de Fargues, Ch Doisy-Dubocra, Ch d'Yquem, Ch Lafaurie-Peyraguey, Ch Liot, Ch Nairac, Ch Raymond-Lafon, Ch Rieussec, Ch St Armand, Ch Sigalas-Rabaud, Ch Suduiraut
Ste-Croix-du-Mont – Ch Loubens, Ch des Coulinats, Ch de Taste
Loupiac – Ch Loupiac-Gaudiet
Premières Côtes de Bordeaux – Ch de Berbec, Ch Reynon
Monbazillac – Ch La Fage

PINOT NOIR
WORLDWIDE

FAMOUS REGION: BURGUNDY

KNOW YOUR GRAPE

It is not surprising that when wine growers think of Pinot Noir, they think of Burgundy. It is, after all, one of the world's greatest red wines and made exclusively from Pinot Noir. Burgundy is like Mount Everest and the fact that Pinot Noir is one of the most difficult grapes in the world to grow successfully, makes it an irresistible challenge. As a wine, it is more refined than the assertive Cabernet Sauvignon, although it often contains higher levels of alcohol. Pinot Noir has a light and sometimes almost rosé colour, except those in Hungary, Australia and California where it assumes a deep red colour.

FLAVOURS

RASPBERRY   CHOCOLATE   JAMMY   VEGETAL

For many wine drinkers, Pinot Noir has the most satisfying tastes of any red wines. In Burgundy they provoke the most exotic descriptions! A splendidly sensuous, velvety series of flavours, often described as raspberry. When young it has some tannin (but far less than Cabernet Sauvignon) which softens quickly.

STYLE

LIGHT ✔   **MEDIUM** ✔   **FULL** ✔

Good alcohol levels but the style is lighter than Cabernet with more noticeable acidity.

IS THE GRAPE NAME ON THE LABEL?

Yes, though often under a synonym – see MAKE THE GRAPE CONNECTION (p.102). Occasionally on the cheapest Burgundies.

HOW MUCH WILL IT COST?

A–D

Most satisfying and characteristic are expensive.

WHEN TO DRINK

The low tannin content makes Pinot Noir ready for drinking sooner than the more tannic wines made from Cabernet Sauvignon and Syrah. Ages well and top quality French Pinot Noirs will last 10 to 30 years.

IS IT OAK-AGED?

As with most classic red wines, oak is widely used for maturing Pinot Noir but, because of the delicate nature of this grape, less so than for Cabernet Sauvignon.

IS IT EVER BLENDED WITH OTHER GRAPES?

Rarely.

KNOW YOUR STYLE

STYLOMETER

Pinot Noir grows best and is closest in style to Burgundy in cool wine regions. Too much heat cuts down the natural acids, producing wines that are too alcoholic with a tendency to bitterness.

LIGHT

GERMANY	Baden, Württemberg, Ahr
FRANCE	Loire, Alsace
NEW ZEALAND	South Island
ITALY	Trentino Alto-Adige

MEDIUM

ITALY	Oltrepo Pavese	
	Friuli-Venezia Giulia	
AUSTRALIA	Tasmania	Pipers Brook
	Victoria	Yarra Valley, Geelong, Bendigo
	Western Australia	Margaret River
FRANCE	Burgundy	Côte de Beaune
USA	California	Carneros, Napa
NEW ZEALAND	North Island	Hawkes Bay, Auckland, Wairarapa

FULL

FRANCE	Burgundy	Côte de Nuits
USA	Oregon	Willamette Valley
SERBIA	Krajina	
HUNGARY	Villany	
SOUTH AFRICA	Overberg	
	Stellenbosch	
AUSTRALIA	South Australia	Adelaide Hills,
	New South Wales	Hunter Valley
ROMANIA	Dealul Mare	

MAKE THE GRAPE CONNECTION

LABELLED BY GRAPE

AUSTRALIA
FRANCE
  Alsace
GERMANY
  (called 'Spätburgunder')
HUNGARY
  (called 'Nagyburgundi')
ITALY
  (sometimes called 'Pinot Nero')
NEW ZEALAND
SERBIA
SOUTH AFRICA
USA
  California
  Oregon
  Washington State

LABELLED BY REGION

FRANCE
  Burgundy
  see BEHIND THE RED BURGUNDY LABEL
    (p.109)
  Côte de Beaune
  Côte Chalonnaise
  Côte de Nuits
  Mâconnais
  Loire
  Menetou-Salon
  Reuilly
  Sancerre

PLAYING THE GAME

Burgundy v The Rest of the World

Pinot Noir and Burgundy are so intimately connected that Burgundy is the obvious benchmark against which to compare all others. It does not mean that Burgundy is best. That is a matter for individual taste.

Game One
Light

Bourgogne Rouge
(a few labels may add 'Pinot Noir')
France

∨

Sancerre Rouge
Loire, France
or
Pinot Noir, New Zealand
South Island,
Marlborough or Canterbury,
or
Pinot Nero, Italy
Trentino Alto-Adige

B–C 3 years from France, 2 years from New Zealand

103

Game Two
Medium

Côte de Beaune
or **Côte de Nuits**
Burgundy

V

Pinot Noir
Australia
or
New Zealand
North Island, Martinborough

Select Pinot Noir from Australia and New Zealand up to 12.5° alcohol.

B–C 3 or 4 years from Burgundy, 2 to 3 from Australia and New Zealand

Game Three
Full

It is sometimes interesting to compare wine at different price levels. The Hungarian wine will be much cheaper than the others, but, if you select it, will it stand up to such illustrious company?

Côte de Beaune
or
Côte de Nuits
Burgundy

V

Pinot Noir
Hungary
Villany
or
USA
California, Carneros or Napa
or
USA
Oregon

Select wines from the USA which are 12.5° or more.

A–D 4 years

WHAT'S ON THE SHELVES

LIGHT

COUNTRY	COMMENTS		
FRANCE **Alsace**	In warmer years successful oak-ageing gives more concentration and body. Often dark pink rather than red in colour. Light flavours of raspberry fruit and acidity. 2 to 6 years	90, 89	B
Loire	Light red wines and delicate pinks from Sancerre, Menetou-Salon and Reuilly. Occasionally matured in oak. Delicate raspberry, some acidity. A little more weight in riper years such as 1990. Young and fresh, 2 to 5 years	90, 88	B–D
GERMANY **Ahr** **Baden** **Württemburg**	Spätburgunder is Germany's pseudonym for Pinot Noir. Some oak-ageing with stylish results. Light, fruity with some sweetness to counterbalance lack of body. Young and fresh, 2 to 4 years	90, 89	A–B
ITALY **Trentino Alto-Adige**	Light, fruity wines but lacking varietal definition. 2 to 4 years	90, 89	A–B
NEW ZEALAND **South Island**	Cool climate and long ripening season mean Pinot Noirs from South Island vineyards have good potential. Smooth and delicate with raspberry, sweet chocolate and vegetal overtones. 2 to 6 years	91, 90 89, 88	C–D

PINOT NOIR – WORLDWIDE

MEDIUM

COUNTRY	COMMENTS		

AUSTRALIA
Victoria
  Bendigo
  Geelong
  Yarra Valley
Tasmania
  Pipers Brook
Western Australia
  Margaret River
	Most of Australia is too hot for the fussy Pinot Noir. These coolest areas begin to produce excellent wines of, or near, Burgundy style. The best have plums and raspberry fruit, with vegetal flavours. The others lack style.
	⊩⊏▭ 2 to 6 years
		91, 90
		89, 88
		87
			B–D

FRANCE **Burgundy**	See BEHIND THE RED BURGUNDY LABEL *(p.109)*.		
ITALY **Friuli-Venezia-** **Giulia** **Oltrepo Pavese**	Light, fruity wine lacking varietal definition. The best are ripe and vegetal, the less successful stewed and jammy. ⊩⊏▭ 2 to 4 years	**90, 89**	**A–B**

NEW ZEALAND
North Island
  Auckland
  Hawke's Bay
  Wairarapa
	The warmer climate produces fuller wines, often with promising potential. Some of the best outside Burgundy. Raspberry, good Pinot Noir character, outstanding from Martinborough (Wairarapa).
	⊩⊏▭ 2 to 6 years
		91, 90
		89, 88
			C–D

USA
California
  Carneros
  Napa
	In cooler areas of Carneros and Napa, wines begin to rival Burgundy with its elegance and smooth vegetal flavours. More substantial than the Côte d'Or.
	⊩⊏▭ 3 to 6 years
		90, 88
		87
			B–D

FULL

COUNTRY	COMMENTS		
AUSTRALIA **New South Wales** Hunter Valley **South Australia** Adelaide Hills	These two areas are not overall best suited to Pinot Noir but some good, full wines are made by the best winemakers *(see p.108)*. Big, full-coloured wines. Cherries and plums in South Australia. Less Pinot Noir character in Hunter Valley. ⟜ 4 to 8 years	**91, 90** **89, 88**	**B–D**
FRANCE **Burgundy**	See BEHIND THE RED BURGUNDY LABEL *(p109)*.		
HUNGARY **Villany**	Hungary's best classic red wine. Oak-aged, inexpensive and delightful. Untypical in colour and style. Deep red and full-bodied. Soft, almost sweet. ⟜ 2 to 4 years		**A**
ROMANIA **Dealul Mare**	Soft, slightly sweet and low in acidity. ⟜ 2 to 3 years		**A**
SERBIA **Krajina**	Not so full or rich as Hungarian Pinot Noirs. Fruity and soft. ⟜ 2 to 4 years		**A**
SOUTH AFRICA **Overberg** **Stellenbosch**	Heat prevents the production of stylish Pinot Noir with two notable exceptions – see SOME RELIABLE PRODUCERS *(p.108)*. Perfumed, cherries and raspberries. ⟜ 4 to 10 years	**91, 90** **89, 88** **87, 86**	**C–D**
USA **Oregon**	The most exciting, established Pinot Noirs outside Burgundy. Oregon's cool climate produces very successful wines, with the best capturing their elegant flavours. Fresh raspberry when young with better acidity balance than California. Developed, ripe vegetal flavours with a sweet finish. ⟜ 3 to 6 years	**90, 88** **87, 86**	**B–D**

RELIABLE PRODUCERS & SHIPPERS

AUSTRALIA
Victoria: Geelong – Balgownie;
Yarra Valley – Coldstream Hills, Lilydale,
Mount Mary, Tarrawarra, Yarra Yering;
Bendigo;
Tasmania: Pipers Brook
Western Australia: Margaret River –
Leeuwin Estate, Moss Wood
New South Wales: Hunter Valley –
Rothbury, Tyrrell
South Australia: Adelaide Hills –
Mountadam

FRANCE
Alsace: Andre Scherer,Heim, Hugel, Jean-Baptiste Adam, Leon Beyer
Burgundy: See BEHIND THE RED BURGUNDY LABEL *(starts opposite)*

GERMANY
Becker, Karl-Heinz Johner, Lingenfelder, Meyer-Nakel

ITALY
Lombardy: Doria, Fontanachiara, Tenuta Mazzolino
Alto-Adige: Tiefenbrunner
Trentino: Cavit, Pojer e Sandri, Vallarom
Friuli: Collavini, Jermann, Russiz Superiore
Veneto: Maculan

NEW ZEALAND
Ata Rangi, Dry River, Gibbston Valley,
Martinborough Vineyards, Matua Valley,
Nobilo, Pallisser Estate, St Helena

SOUTH AFRICA
Hamilton-Russell Vineyards, Meerlust

USA
California: Acacia, Calera, Chalone, Clos du Bois, Edna Valley Vineyards, Firestone Vineyard, Hanzell, Robert Mondavi, Saintsbury, Sanford, Trefethen, ZD Wines
Oregon: Adelsheim, Eyrie Vineyards, Knudsen Erath, Ponzi, Sokol Blosser, Tualatin

BEHIND THE RED BURGUNDY LABEL
PINOT NOIR & GAMAY

PINOT NOIR KNOW YOUR GRAPE

To qualify for the right to use the name Burgundy, red wines must be made from one of two grapes: Pinot Noir and Gamay. Pinot Noir is the king and used exclusively to make the best wines in the northern regions. Although Gamay is not a classic variety, we include it because it produces the well known wines of Beaujolais, the most southerly Burgundian wine region. Gamay is rarely used in any other region except the Mâconnais.

Red Burgundy (excluding Beaujolais) is one of the most evocative wine names, so famous – and expensive – that it has become the benchmark for Pinot Noir

winegrowers all over the world who aspire to greatness. Really great Burgundy from Pinot Noir is made on average only twice in a decade. In the preceding worldwide guide, we explained how difficult it is, even in the most favourable climates of the world, to match Burgundy's Pinot Noir taste.

Although often pale in colour, Burgundy is deceptively high in alcohol. As the grapes are often not ripe enough to achieve an acceptable level of alcohol, sugar is added in most years (legally) to increase the strength *(see CHAPTALISATION on p.205)*.

FLAVOURS

(LEAF MOULD) (TRUFFLES) (CHOCOLATE) (RASPBERRIES) (CHERRIES)

A gamut of flavours and smells send wine writers reaching for their dictionaries.

STYLE

LIGHT   **MEDIUM**   **FULL**

✔   ✔   ✔

IS IT EVER BLENDED WITH OTHER GRAPES?

Only to make the undistinguished, ordinary 'Bourgogne Passetoutgrain'.

HOW MUCH WILL IT COST?

A–D

Basic wines band **A**, the better village wines bands **B–C**. The really great wines band **D**.

IS IT OAK-AGED?

Yes. Most wines are fermented in stainless steel tanks, then matured in small oak barrels.

WHEN TO DRINK

The vintage is very important.
See VINTAGES *(p.119)*.

IS THE GRAPE NAME ON THE LABEL?

Hardly ever. Only on very basic wines.

KNOW YOUR STYLE

The two regions are the Côte d'Or, comprising the Côte de Nuits and the Côte de Beaune, and the Côte Chalonnaise.

Côte d'Or: Côte de Nuits wines are full flavoured with enought tannin to give backbone but not enough to be aggressive. Côte de Beaune wines have more elegance and are lighter and more stylish.

Côte Chalonnaise: These wines lack the elegance of Côte d'Or but are excellent value for money.

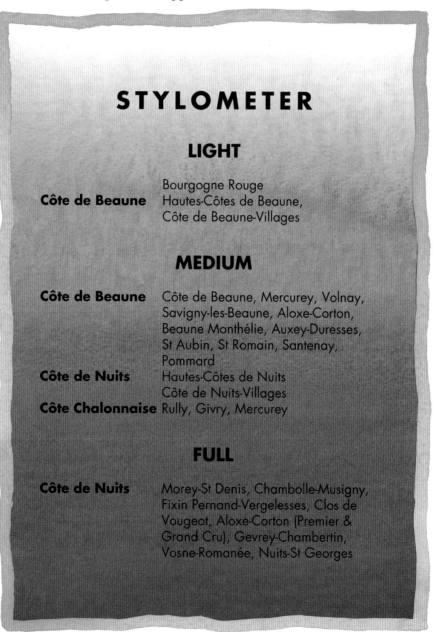

STYLOMETER

LIGHT

Côte de Beaune	Bourgogne Rouge Hautes-Côtes de Beaune, Côte de Beaune-Villages

MEDIUM

Côte de Beaune	Côte de Beaune, Mercurey, Volnay, Savigny-les-Beaune, Aloxe-Corton, Beaune Monthélie, Auxey-Duresses, St Aubin, St Romain, Santenay, Pommard
Côte de Nuits	Hautes-Côtes de Nuits Côte de Nuits-Villages
Côte Chalonnaise	Rully, Givry, Mercurey

FULL

Côte de Nuits	Morey-St Denis, Chambolle-Musigny, Fixin Pernand-Vergelesses, Clos de Vougeot, Aloxe-Corton (Premier & Grand Cru), Gevrey-Chambertin, Vosne-Romanée, Nuits-St Georges

MAKE THE GRAPE CONNECTION

Thanks to the Burgundian laws of inheritance, vineyards are split between many owners – the average holding is only four hectares – but, good or bad, all are allowed to use the name of their region, village or vineyard on their labels. So, more than for any other wines, it is very important to know the names of reputable producers and merchants.

APPELLATION CONTROLEE

As with white Burgundy, there are five levels of AC for Pinot Noir wines. The smaller the area, the more expensive and supposedly finer the wines. Do remember that the AC is a guarantee of origin, not necessarily of quality. Sadly, too much red Burgundy is of average quality and overpriced.

GRAND CRU
VINEYARDS
The crème de la crème

PREMIER CRU VINEYARDS
The second flight of single vineyards

VILLAGES WITHIN REGIONS
Specific villages. Best quality before Premier & Grand Cru

REGIONS WITHIN BURGUNDY
Sound everyday wines from the Côtes de Beaune & Nuits and Chalonnaise

BURGUNDY
The whole area, the basic AC

The names on the label will indicate whether the wine comes from Burgundy, from a specific region, a named village or a vineyard within a village.

REGION	LABELLED AS
BURGUNDY i.e.the main area	Bourgogne Rouge
REGIONS WITHIN BURGUNDY	Hautes-Côtes de Beaune, Hautes-Côtes de Nuits, Côtes de Beaune-Villages, Côtes de Nuits-Villages, Côte de Beaune

VILLAGES WITHIN THE REGIONS

Côte de Beaune	Auxey-Duresses, Beaune, Chassagne-Montrachet, Monthélie, Pernand-Vergelesses, Pommard, St Aubin, St Romain, Santenay, Savigny-les-Beaune, Volnay
Côte de Chalonnaise	Givry, Mercurey, Rully
Côte de Nuits	Chambolle-Musigny, Fixin, Flagey-Echézeaux, Gevrey-Chambertin, Marsannay, Morey-St-Denis, Nuits-St Georges, Vosne-Romanée, Vougeot

The finest vineyards have their own ACs. Illogically, Premier Cru are outranked by Grand Cru vineyards.

PREMIER CRU VINEYARDS

Must include village name on the label, e.g. Chambolle-Musigny Les Amoureux

COTE DE BEAUNE

Aloxe-Corton: Les Maréchaudes

Auxey-Duresses: Les Duresses, La Val

Beaune: Bressandes, Cent Vignes, Champimonts, Les Fèves, Les Grèves, Marconnets, Clos de la Mousse, Clos des Mouches, Clos du Roi, Les Teurons, Les Vignes Franches

Chassagne-Montrachet: La Boudriotte, Le Morgeot, Clos St Jean

Monthélie: Les Champs-Fulliot

Pernand-Vergelesses: Ile des Vergelesses

Pommard: Grands Epenots, Les Rugiens

Savigny-les-Beaune: La Dominodes, Les Lavières, Les Hauts Marconnets

Volnay: Caillerets, Champans, Clos des Chênes, Chevrets, Santenots

COTE DE NUITS

Chambolle-Musigny: Les Amoureux, Les Charmes

Fixin: Les Arvelets, Clos du Chapitre, Les Hervelets, Les Maix-Bas, Clos Napoléon, Clos de la Perrière

Flagey-Echézeaux and Vosne Romanée: Les Beaumonts, Les Brûlées, Les Chaumes, Les Gaudichots, La Grande Rue, Aux Malconsorts, Les Suchots

Gevrey-Chambertin: Cazeliers, Champeaux, Champonnets, Clos-Prieur, Combes-aux-Moines, Combottes, Etournelles, Fonteny, Lavaux-St Jacques, Clos St Jacques, Les Varoilles

Morey-St Denis: Clos-Bussières, Charmes, Clos-des-Ormes, Les Sorbés

Nuits St Georges: Aux Chaignots, Les Porets, Les Pruliers, La Richemone, Les St Georges, Les Vaucrains

Vougeot: Clos Blanc, Les Cras, Clos de la Perrière, Les Petits Vougeot

GRAND CRU VINEYARDS

These do not have to show the village name, e.g. the famous Le Musigny vineyard does not add the village name Chambolle-Musigny.

COTE DE BEAUNE

Aloxe-Corton: Le Corton, Corton-Bressandes, Corton-Clos du Roi, Corton-Maréchaudes

COTE DE NUITS

Chambolle-Musigny: Bonnes-Mares, Le Musigny

Flagey-Echézeaux and Vosne-Romanée: Echézeaux, Grands Echézeaux, La Tâche, La Romanée, Romanée-Conti, Romanée-St Vivant

Gevrey-Chambertin: Chambertin, Clos de Bèze, Chapelle-Chambertin, Charmes-Chambertin, Latricières-Chambertin, Mazis-Chambertin, Ruchottes-Chambertin

Morey-St Denis: Clos des Lambreys, Clos de la Roche, Clos St Denis, Clos de Tart

Vougeot: Clos de Vougeot

PLAYING THE GAME

There are endless permutations you can make to reveal the marvels of Pinot Noir. There are so many different tastes and flavours from areas so close to each other. Sometimes it is a matter of only a few hundred yards. Which will suit you best? **NB:** With Burgundy, it is important to refer to the vintages *(see p.119)* and list of reliable producers and merchants when choosing the wines *(see p.116)*

Game One
Which Region?

There's often £2 or more difference between wines from the fashionable Côte d'Or (Côte de Beaune and Côte de Nuits) and the Côte Chalonnaise. Is the reputation of the Côte d'Or worth the extra price tag?

Cote d'Or

Nuits St Georges
or
Beaune

 B–C   5 years +

Cote Chalonnaise

𝒱

Mercurey
or
Rully

Game Two
Which Village?

This is where comparative tasting of Burgundy becomes expensive. At village level, prices start to escalate. Are the wines worth it? Will you find the Côte de Beaune lighter and more elegant than the Côte de Nuits? Which do you prefer?

Cote de Nuits   *Cote de Beaune*

Gevrey-Chambertin		**Savigny-les-Beaune**
or	**V**	or
Fixin		**Pommard**

 C–D 🔑 4 years +

Game Three
Which Vineyards?

The Premier and Grand Cru vineyards are considerably more expensive than the village wines and the taste should justify the price.

Premier or Grand Cru Vineyards

Côte de Nuits	**V**	**Côte de Beaune**

Choose any Premier or Grand Cru wines from the list on p.119 and see which Côte you prefer at this exalted level.

C–D 🔑 not less than 5 years

WHAT'S ON THE SHELVES

The weather plays a vital role in Burgundy and vintages are therefore all-important.
A general guide to the style and character of recent vintages *(see p.119)*.

LIGHT

REGION	COMMENTS	
Côte de Beaune-Villages	Good Pinot character and the soft style of Beaune. 3 to 5 years	**B**
Hautes-Côtes de Beaune	An area to watch as the prices for better known names continue to escalate. Wines with a pretty red colour and attractive floral smell. 3 to 5 years	**A–B**

MEDIUM

REGION	COMMENTS	
Aloxe-Corton **Côte de Beaune**	The wines have more tannin than most Côte de Beaune wines, so age well. The village has the only Grand Cru in the Côte de Beaune – Corton – which produces magnificent, powerful, almost tannic wines. Rich flavour, some say with truffles. 3 to 10 years	**B–D**
Auxey-Duresses **Côte de Beaune**	Rather hard when young but developing into fruity wines with raspberry flavour. 4 to 8 years	**B–C**
Beaune **Côte de Beaune**	After Nuits St Georges, the best known name in Burgundy. Good, honest wines, good varietal flavours. 4 to 10 years	**B–D**
Côte de Beaune	AC restricted to wines grown round Beaune only. Usually more elegant versions of Côte de Beaune-Villages 3 to 6 years	**B–C**
Côte de Nuits-Villages	Wines worth watching. Good style and Côte de Nuits character. 3 to 8 years	**B**
Givry **Côte Chalonnaise**	Delicate, fragrant wines 3 to 6 years	**B**

BEHIND THE RED BURGUNDY LABEL – PINOT NOIR

REGION	COMMENTS	
Hautes-Côtes de Nuits	Excellent value wines with good fruit and style of the Côte de Nuits. ⌖ 3 to 6 years	**B**
Mercurey **Côte Chalonnaise**	The best of the Chalonnais reds with depth and some complexity. Earthy taste, this time with cherries added. ⌖ 3 to 8 years	**B–C**
Monthélie **Côte de Beaune**	Usually very good value. Pretty, scented wines, medium full. ⌖ 3 to 6 years	**B–C**
Pommard **Côte de Beaune**	One of the better known villages because it is easy to pronounce! Considered the fullest and most powerful of the Côte de Beaune wines. Deep colour, smell of violets. ⌖ 4 to 10 years	**B–C**
Rully **Côte Chalonnaise**	Generally light in colour. Earthy flavour tinged with raspberries and nuts. ⌖ 3 to 6 years	**B**
St Aubin **Côte de Beaune**	Wines to watch. Slightly lighter versions of the great red wines of Chassagne-Montrachet. Strawberries. ⌖ 3 to 8 years	**B–C**
St Romain **Côte de Beaune**	Fruity wines, strawberries and cherries with added earthy taste. ⌖ 3 to 8 years	**B**
Santenay **Côte de Beaune**	Quite tannic when young with a flavour of strawberries and almonds. ⌖ 4 to 8 years	**B–C**
Savigny-les-Beaune **Côte de Beaune**	Usually the lightest of the Beaune village wines. Scented wines, easy to drink. Floral, with red fruit flavours. ⌖ 3 to 8 years	**B–C**
Volnay **Côte de Beaune**	Elegant and fragrant wines with excellent balance. Violets and redcurrants. ⌖ 3 to 8 years	**B–C**

FULL

REGION	COMMENTS

Chambolle-Musigny
Côte de Nuits

Much stronger wines than their apparent delicacy suggests. Fruity, raspberry flavour with spicy background.
5 to 10 years

B–D

Chassagne-Montrachet
Côte de Beaune

A rare red wine from a predominantly white area.
5 to 10 years

C–D

Gevrey-Chambertin
Côte de Nuits

The 'ordinary' village wines are invariably overpriced and, sadly, usually characterless. However, there are a clutchful of Premiers Crus and more Grands Crus than in any other village. These top wines are firm, tannic, almost severe when young but maturing into beautifully balanced wines, full of colour, body and aroma. Almost every description is used for Gevrey wines, from raspberries and strawberries to cherries and game!
5 to 10 years

C–D

Fixin
Côte de Nuits

Quite strong wines with good colour and some tannin. Blackcurrants rather than strawberries. Some find a gamey flavour.
4 to 8 years

B–D

Morey-St Denis
Côte de Nuits

There are five Grand Crus in this village. Considered the lightest of the Côte de Nuits wines. Firm and well structured with cherry and redcurrant flavours.
4 to 10 years

B–D

Nuits-St Georges
Côte de Nuits

The best-known name in Burgundy and the home of some of its best wines. Full colour, fragrant almost spicy smell and blackcurrant flavour. Quite high in tannin, so firm and long-lived.
4 to 10 years

B–D

**Vosne-Romanée &
Flagey-Echézeaux**
Côte de Nuits

These villages hold the crème de la crème of Grands Crus. Deep, rich, velvety wines, strongly perfumed with every flavour under the sun.
Wines of great delicacy.
5 to 10 years +

C–D

Vougeot
Côte de Nuits

The straightforward village wines are pleasant enough but it is the Premiers Crus and particularly the Grand Cru, Clos de Vougeot, which make this village famous. Clos de Vougeot should be full and rich, chocolatey with a floral smell but, with over 70 owners, style varies.
4 to 10 years

C–D

VINTAGES

(Côte d'Or, Côte Chalonnaise)

1978
Very great vintage. Top wines still have many years of life ahead of them. Very expensive.

1982
Soft, easy-drinking wines, certainly at their peak now. Given the right producer, you should get some very enjoyable bottles.

1983
Very tannic wines. The fruit is dying out in some wines but best really need another ten years in the bottle before they are ready to drink. If you can wait that long, you should get some really heavy rich wines.

1984
Lightweight year, with high acidity. If the price is not too high – and the producer is right – there could be some bargains around for drinking now.

1985
Potentially very great year. At the moment, there is too much tannin to taste the fruit, so it looks as though we will have a long wait for these wines to be drinkable.

1986
Middle-of-the-road vintage. Some wines taste too tough, and will never be great. Best producers have made some fine wines but perhaps not as good as 1985.

1987
Another mixed bag. Burgundy is always like this. Good producers have made wines that are deep, rich, but dry with plenty of fruit and which need keeping for ten years at least.

1988
Early days yet, but signs are that this will be one of the fruitiest vintages of the 1980s, with wines of excellent colour. May not last as long as 1985s or 1987s, but may be more enjoyable.

1989
Lighter in colour and fruit than 1988, but could be wines for earlier drinking, possibly even by mid-1990s.

1990
In style somewhere between 1988 and 1989. Wines have good colour, more tannin than 1989s, but good balancing acidity. They have pleasing raspberry flavours.

1991
What might have been a great vintage has turned out to be patchy in quality and lcw in quantity. Some good wines will be made but this will never be a great vintage.

RELIABLE PRODUCERS & SHIPPERS

PRODUCERS

COTE DE BEAUNE

Aloxe-Corton: Adrien Belland, Antonin Guyon, Bonneaux de Martray, Chandon de Briailles, Chevalier, Daniel Senard, Dubreuil-Fontaine, Hubert Bouzereau-Gruère, Louis Chapuis, Michel Gaunoux, Michel Voarick, Moillard, Parent, Rapet, Tollot-Beaut, Tollot-Voarick,

Auxey-Duresses: Bernard Roy, du Duc de Magenta, Henri Latour, Jean-Pierre Diconne, Leroy, Michel Prunier

Beaune: Albert Morey, Albert Morot, Arnoux Père et Fils, Besancenot-Mathouillet, Bernard Delagrange, Chantal Lescure, Jacques Germain, Jacques Prieur, Joseph Drouhin, Machard de Gramont, Michel Lafarge, Moillard, Mussy, Parent, Robert et Michel Ampeau, Tollot-Beaut

Blagny: de Blagny, Joseph Matrot, Robert Ampeau

Chassagne-Montrachet: Albert-Bernard Morey, Bachalet-Ramonet, Domaine Carillon, Gagnard-Delagrange, Ramonet-Prudhon

Chorey-lès-Beaune: Jacques Germain, Tollot-Beaut

Monthélie: A Ropiteau-Mignon, Château de Monthélie, Eric Boussey, Eric de Suremain, Henri Potinet-Ampeau, Jacques Boigelot

Pernand-Vergelesses: Antonin Guyon, Besancenot-Mathouillet, Bonneau du Martray, Chandon de Briailles, Chapuis, Denis Père et Fils, Dubreuil-Fontaine, Jacques Germain, Laleure-Piot,Maurice Rollin et Fils, Michel Voarick, Rapet Père et Fils

Pommard: Bernard Delagrange, Comte Armand, de Courcel, de Montille, Guillemard-Dupont et ses Fils, Henri Boillot, Lejeune, Louis Glantenay, Machard de Gramont, Michael Gaunoux, Mussy, Parent, Puthier-Rieusset, Robert et Michel Ampeau

St-Romain: Alain Gras, du Château de Puligny-Montrachet, René Gras Boisson, René Thévenin-Monthélie, Taupenot Père et Fils

St-Aubin: Aimé Langoureau, André Moingeon, Clerget, Gérard Thomas, Henri Prudhon et Fils, Lamy, Marc Colin, Madame Jean Bachelt, Michel Lamanthe, Roux Père et Fils

Santenay: Adrien Belland, Bernard Morey, Ch de la Charrière, de l'Abbaye de Santenay, de la Pousse d'Or, des Hautes-Cornières, Guy Dufouleur, Fleurot-Larose, Hervé Olivier, Hubert Bouzereau, Jean Giradin, Lequin-Roussot, Mestre-Père et Fils, Michel Clair, Prieur-Brunet, Prosper Mafoux, Roux, St-Michel

Savigny-lès-Beaune: Antonin Guyon, Capron-Manieux, Chandon de Briailles, G Girard-Vollot, Henri Boillot, Jean-Marc Pavelot, Parent, Pavelot-Glantenay, Pierre Guillemot, Simon Bize, Tollot-Beaut

Volnay: Bernard Delagrange, Bernard Glantenay, Bitouzet Prieur, de la Pousse d'Or, de Montille, les Comtes Lafon, Louis Glantenay, Marquis d-Angerville, Michel Lafarge, Pierre Boillot, Y Clerget

COTE CHALONNAISE

Givry: Bernard Tatraux, de la Renarde, du Gardin, Gérard Mouton, Jean Chofflet, Joblot, Lumpp Frères, Michel Derain, Propriété Desvignes, Ragot, Thénard

Mercurey: de la Monette, de Suremain, du Prieuré, François Portheau et Fils, Jeannin-Naltet Père et Fils, Louis Menand Père et Fils, Luc Brintet et Frédéric Charles, Marceau, Maréchal, Michel Juillot, Saier, Yves et Paul de Launay,

Rully: Belleville, de la Folie, de la Renarde, du Prieuré, Guy Mugnier, H et P Jacqueson, Jean-Claude Brelière, Jean Coulon, Pierre Cogny

COTE D'OR/COTE DE NUITS

Chambolle-Musigny: Alain Hudelot-Noëllat, Bernard Amiot, Bernard Serveau, Clair-Daü, Comte Georges de Vogüe, Daniel

Moine-Hudelot, Drouhin-Laroze, G Barthod-Noëllat, Georges Roumier et Fils, Jacques-Fréderic Mugnier

Fixin: André Bart, Bruno Clair, Domaine Mongeard-Mugneret, Philippe Jolie, Pierre Gelin, Vincent et Denis Berthaut

Flagey-Echézeaux: de la Romanée-Conti, Henri Jayer, Jacqueline Jayer, Mongeard-Mugneret, Robert Sirugue

Gevrey-Chambertin: Alain Burguet, Armand Rousseau, Bernard Bachelet, Bernard Maume, Clair-Daü, Domaine Rossignol-Trapet, Drouhin-Laroze, du Ch de Beaune, Dujac, Gabriel Tortochot, G Roumier, Henri Magnien, Jean Taupenot, Joseph Roty, Labouré-Roi, Lucien Boillot, Pernot-Fourrier, Philippe Leclerc, Pierre Damoy, Ponsot

Hautes Côtes de Nuits: Bernard Hudelot/de Montmain, Ch Mandelot, François Charles, Guy Dufouleur, Jean Joliot et Fils, Les Caves des Hautes Côtes, Lucien Jacob, Michel Serveau, Naudin, Thévenot-le Brun et Fils

Marsannay: André Bart, Bruno Clair, Charles Quillardet, Clair-Daü, Jean Fournier, Huguenot Père et Fils, Philippe Charlopin-Parizot, René Bouvier

Morey-St Denis: Arlaud Père et Fils, Armand Rousseau, Bernard Serveau, Clair-Daü, Dujac, Georges Bryczek, Georges Lignier, G Roumier, J Truchot-Martin, Lambrays, Pierre Amiot, Ponsot, Ropiteau

Nuits-St Georges: Alain Michelot, Charles Viénot, Daniel Rion, Gris, Henri Gouges, Henri Jayer, Henri Remoriquet, Hospice de Nuits, Jacqueline Jayer, Jean Grivot, Machard de Gramont, Manière-Noirot, Moillard, Robert Chevillon, Robert Dubois et Fils, Xavier Liger-Belair

Vosne-Romanée: Alain Hudelot-Noëllat, Daniel Bissey, Daniel Rion, de la Romanée-Conti, de la SCI du Ch de Vosne-Romanée, Jean Grivot, Jean Gros, Jacqueline Jayer, Lamarche, Manière-Noirot, Moillard, Mongeard-Mugneret, Robert Arnoux

Vougeot: Bertagna, Daniel Rion, Deroubaix-Indelli, Drouhin-Laroze, Georges Clerget, G Rounier, Jean Grivot, Jean Gros, Mongeard-Mugneret, Robert Armoux

SHIPPERS

The shipper buys wine from growers throughout Burgundy, matures it in his own cellars and labels it under his own name: Bouchard Père et Fils, Chanson Père et Fils, B & J-M Delaunay, Drouhin, Faiveley, Louis Jadot, Louis Latour.

GAMAY
KNOW YOUR GRAPE

Gamay is Beaujolais, but you would not know it because, although Beaujolais is the largest red wine area in Burgundy, the grape name rarely appears on the labels. This is the same as in the Mâconnais, where 30% of the production is red wine and almost entirely Gamay.

At its most basic, Gamay makes a quaffing wine. Cheap and cheerful, pretty to look at and easy to drink with a delicious raspberry flavour. A perfect description for everyday Beaujolais. How sad that its reputation is tarnished by Beaujolais Nouveau. Overpriced, overpublicised and over here.

The basic wines are labelled Beaujolais and you should drink them as young as possible, up to two years. Some 39 villages are entitled to the name Beaujolais Villages. These wines *should* have more fruit and depth than plain Beaujolais but are often undistinguished and overpriced.

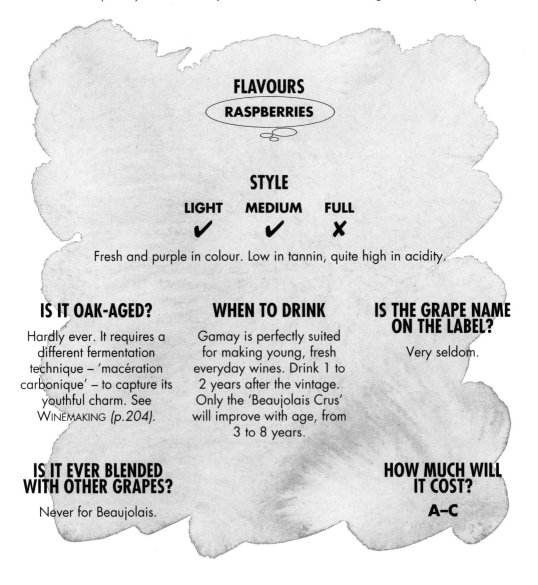

FLAVOURS
RASPBERRIES

STYLE

LIGHT	MEDIUM	FULL
✔	✔	✘

Fresh and purple in colour. Low in tannin, quite high in acidity.

IS IT OAK-AGED?

Hardly ever. It requires a different fermentation technique – 'macération carbonique' – to capture its youthful charm. See WINEMAKING *(p.204)*.

WHEN TO DRINK

Gamay is perfectly suited for making young, fresh everyday wines. Drink 1 to 2 years after the vintage. Only the 'Beaujolais Crus' will improve with age, from 3 to 8 years.

IS THE GRAPE NAME ON THE LABEL?

Very seldom.

IS IT EVER BLENDED WITH OTHER GRAPES?

Never for Beaujolais.

HOW MUCH WILL IT COST?

A–C

KNOW YOUR STYLE

There are two main Gamay regions in Burgundy, Beaujolais and Mâconnais.

Beaujolais is the largest of Burgundy's red wine regions and 100% Gamay. The Beaujolais Crus come from the northern section. 'Everyday' Beaujolais, for want of a better description, comes from the southern section and is lower in tannin, hence the early drinking.

In the Mâconnais only 30% of production is red and mainly Gamay.

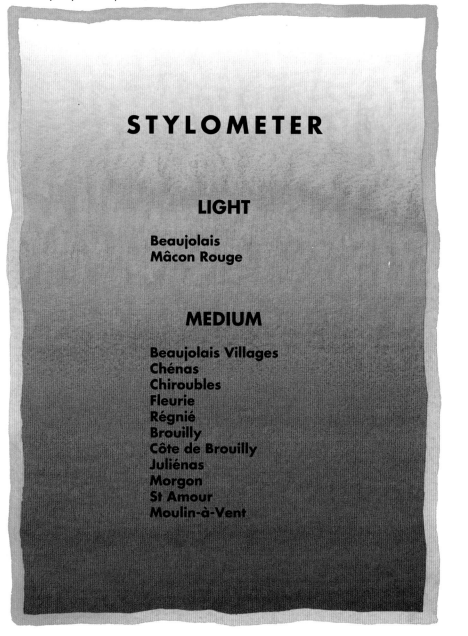

STYLOMETER

LIGHT

Beaujolais
Mâcon Rouge

MEDIUM

Beaujolais Villages
Chénas
Chiroubles
Fleurie
Régnié
Brouilly
Côte de Brouilly
Juliénas
Morgon
St Amour
Moulin-à-Vent

MAKE THE GRAPE CONNECTION

APPELLATION CONTROLEE

There are only three levels of Appellation Contrôlée in Beaujolais:

BEAUJOLAIS CRUS
10 named villages

BEAUJOLAIS VILLAGES
39 villages qualify for this AC.
The wines are often a blend of the villages.
The names seldom appear on the label

THE MAIN AREA i.e. **BEAUJOLAIS**
Basic Beaujolais including Beaujolais Nouveau.
Most Beaujolais falls into this category.

The name Gamay will rarely be shown on Beaujolais labels.
The Beaujolais Crus villages are all listed in WHAT'S ON THE SHELVES (p.127).

PLAYING THE GAME

Game One
Which Grape?

First, which of the two major grape varieties do you prefer?

Pinot Noir

Côtes de Beaune or
Côtes de Nuits

✓

Gamay

basic Beaujolais
(not a Beaujolais Nouveau)

B   Pinot Noir 3 years, Gamay 2 years

Game Two
Gamay

Now compare the different styles of Gamay.

Cheap & Cheerful

basic Beaujolais

✓

Serious

Fleurie or **Brouilly**

A–C   2 years

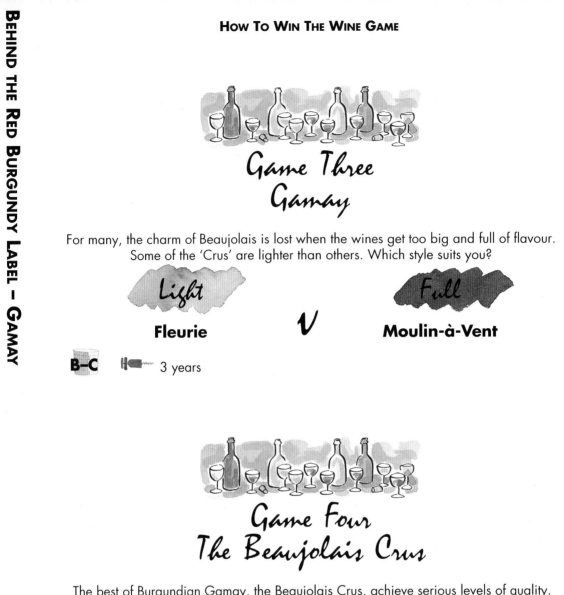

Game Three
Gamay

For many, the charm of Beaujolais is lost when the wines get too big and full of flavour. Some of the 'Crus' are lighter than others. Which style suits you?

Light   **v**   *Full*

Fleurie   **Moulin-à-Vent**

B–C   🍷   3 years

Game Four
The Beaujolais Crus

The best of Burgundian Gamay, the Beaujolais Crus, achieve serious levels of quality. The wines provide a range of different tastes and flavours. You will taste some of the more noticeable when comparing:

St Amour   **v**   **Morgon**

or   or

Brouilly   **Juliénas**

B–C   🍷   3 years

WHAT'S ON THE SHELVES

LIGHT

COUNTRY	COMMENTS	
Beaujolais **Beaujolais**	Should be cheap and cheerful, for this is a wine for quenching the thirst or washing down the food. Sadly, too many are now overpriced. Supérieure only means an additional degree of alcohol; the style remains light. Purple colour and flavours of cherries and raspberries. Delicious when drunk young and fresh, even chilled. 1 to 2 years	A–B
Mâcon Rouge **Mâconnais**	The Gamay grape does not give of its best in the Mâconnais and the red wines are usually dull and ordinary without any of the zest of Beaujolais. 1 to 2 years	A

MEDIUM
The Beaujolais Crus
(in alphabetical order)

Beaujolais Villages	39 villages are entitled to this AC. Sometimes, it is safer to spend a few pence more and buy a wine which actually names the village. They have the colour and flavour of true Gamay and should be better than plain Beaujolais. 2 to 4 years	B
Brouilly	The largest production of the Crus. Straightforward, pleasing wines for drinking young. Fresh peaches. 2 to 5 years	B–C

BEHIND THE RED BURGUNDY LABEL – GAMAY

COUNTRY	COMMENTS	
Chénas	Not the best known of the Crus. Lacking in charm. Plummy. 2 to 4 years	**B–C**
Chiroubles	Drunk mainly in France where it is very popular for drinking young. The lightest of the Crus with a cherry flavour. 2 to 4 years	**B–C**
Côte de Brouilly	Firm, big wines, full of fruit but lacking elegance. 2 to 5 years	**B–C**
Fleurie	The Cru with one of the biggest yields. Easy-to-drink wines, full of cherry flavour. 2 to 4 years	**B–C**
Juliénas	Good firm wines with more tannin and acidity than most of the Crus. 2 to 5 years	**B–C**
Morgon	Big production. Wild cherries. Ages well to become Pinot Noir-like. 2 to 6 years	**B–C**
Moulin-à-Vent	The fullest of the Crus; can be laid down. Good colour, fruit and tannin. 3 to 8 years	**B–C**
Régnié	Newly created as a Cru and the least distinguished. Decent, fresh wines but seldom better than many plain Beaujolais Villages. In taste, a minor version of Brouilly. 2 to 4 years	**B–C**
St Amour	Delicate wines which last well in the bottle. Raspberries and peaches. 2 to 6 years	**B–C**

BEAUJOLAIS VINTAGES

(Older vintages are only relevant for the Beaujolais Crus)

1985
Greatest Beaujolais vintage of the 1980s, and one where the Cru Beaujolais – and even some Beaujolais Villages – are full of fruit and life, and are just turning into a rich mellowness.

1986
Very little pleasure here. In fact it would be difficult to find any wines left in the shops.

1987
Another good year for Beaujolais, though lighter than 1985. Most of the Beaujolais and Beaujolais Villages should have been drunk by now, but Beaujolais Cru wines are still attractive. Especially Chiroubles, Moulin-à-Vent and Julienas.

1988
Yet again, a good year in Beaujolais. Here, though, it is more patchy and producers' names are important. Most of the Beaujolais Crus wines are good, especially from Domaines, but are not great keepers.

1989
A very early harvest and a good one. Good fruity wines but they have matured quickly. The Beaujolais Crus will be at their prime in 1993.

1990
Another successful year for Beaujolais – the fourth in a row – varying in quality from good to very good. Overall the wines have good fruit.

1991
Unlike the Côte d'Or, 1991 was a happy year for Beaujolais. Full, rich wines not unlike the 1989s and close to their quality.

RELIABLE PRODUCERS & SHIPPERS

Beaujolais-Villages
Ch de Corcelles, Ch de la Grand Grange, Ch la Tour Bourdon, Ch Varennes, de Montmeron, H Monternot et Fils, Joubert, St-Sorlin,

Brouilly
André Ronzière, Ch de la Chaize, Ch de Pierreux, Ch du Bluizard, Claudius Geoffray, de Combillaty, de la Roche, de Vuril, Georges Dutraive, Patrick Vermorel, Robert Condemine, Robert Farjat, Ruet

Chénas
Ch Bonnet, Ch de Chénas, Daniel Robin, Guy Braillon, Hubert Lapierre, Jean-Louis Santé, Louis Champagnon, Manoir des Journets, Michel Crozet,

Chiroubles
Bouillard, Ch de Raousset, Cheysson-les-Farges, de Javernand, de Moulin, Desmure Père et Fils, des Vignerons à Chiroubles, Georges Passot, La Maison Gérard-Roger Méziat, René Savoye

Côte de Brouilly
André Large, Ch Thivin, de Chavanne, de Conroy, du Petit Pressoir, Lucien et Robert Verger

Fleurie
Caves des Producteurs de Fleurie, Ch de Grand Pré, de la Presle, de Montgenas, des Quatre Vents, du Point du Jour, Maurice Bruone, Michel Chignard

Juliénas
André Pelletier, Ch de Juliénas, Ch des Capitans, Ch des Poupets, Claude et Michell Joubet, de la Seigneurie de Juliénas, Ernest Aujas, Gonon, Jacques Perrachon, Monnet, Raymond et Michel Tête

Morgon
Ch de Pizay, de Colonat, de la Chanise, de Ruyère, des Pillets, Georges Brun, Jacques Trichard, Jean Descombes, Lieven, Louis Desvignes, Louis Genillon, Savoye, Sylvain Fessy

Moulin-à-Vent
Alphonse Mortet, Ch de Jacques, Ch du Moulin-à-Vent, Ch Portier, Chauvet Frères, Clos du Moulin-à-Vent, de la Tour du Bief, des Caves, Héritiers Finaz Devillaine, Jacky Janodet, Jean Brugne-Le Vivier, Lemonon, Louis Champagnon, Moulin-à-Vent Hospices, Raymond Siffert

Régnie
Ch de la Tour Bourdon, de la Gerarde, Desplace Frères, Jean et Yves Durand, Joël Rochette

St-Amour
Ch de St-Amour, de Mongrin, des Billards, des Duc, Dufour, du Paradis, Elie Mongénie, Francis Saillant, Guy Patissier, Janin, Jean Patissier

CABERNET SAUVIGNON
WORLDWIDE

FAMOUS REGION: BORDEAUX, FRANCE

KNOW YOUR GRAPE

Cabernet Sauvignon produces the world's best known and currently most fashionable red wines, and every serious wine-producing country now exports them. All have a strong family resemblance, not least their high tannin content and rigid, firm character. In warm regions, where the grapes become fully ripe, the wines mature quite quickly and are drinkable sooner. In the cooler climates of northern Europe – Bordeaux in particular – Cabernet Sauvignon ripens later and takes years to lose its austere nature. Therefore it is blended with the softer, quicker ripening Merlot which makes the wines ready for drinking earlier.

This guide focuses on Cabernet Sauvignon. However, together with the following guide on MERLOT, they lead to BEHIND THE BORDEAUX LABEL. This explains how varying percentages of these two varieties produce quite different tastes.

FLAVOURS

MINT   HERBS   CEDARWOOD   BLACKCURRANT   EUCALYPTUS

The main characteristic is the deep colour and concentrated smell and taste of blackcurrants, but there are all sorts of other flavours.

STYLE

LIGHT	MEDIUM	FULL
✔	✔	✔

Cabernet Sauvignon is rather like a guardsman on parade: severe, upright and firm, only softening with age, a process which is speeded up in warm climates. Obvious high tannin content makes these wines slow to develop but long-lived and is most noticeable from cool climates. So if you do not like too much tannin, try Australia and the Americas.

WHEN TO DRINK

Drink the lightest and cheapest from 2 to 4 years. The more expensive from 3 to 8 years and more.

IS THE GRAPE NAME ON THE LABEL?

Usually – see MAKE THE GRAPE CONNECTION *(p.134)* for the exceptions.

HOW MUCH WILL IT COST?
A–D

IS IT EVER BLENDED WITH OTHER GRAPES?

In Bordeaux virtually the whole crop is blended with Merlot. Other winemakers are increasingly using the Bordeaux mix. In Australia, Shiraz is often used to vary the taste.

IS IT OAK-AGED?

Cabernet Sauvignon responds well to oak-ageing, normal practice in all but the cheapest wines. In Bordeaux and most of Europe, oak is used with subtlety. Worldwide, oak flavouring tends to be more overt but in Australia and California many of the better winemakers are using less oak to produce a more elegant style.

KNOW YOUR STYLE

STYLOMETER

As Cabernet Sauvignon is a late-ripening variety, warm climates produce the ripest fruit and thus, easy-to-drink wines.

LIGHT

NEW ZEALAND	South Island	Marlborough
ITALY	Trentino Alto-Adige	
	Friuli-Venezia-Giulia	
AUSTRALIA	Tasmania	
	Victoria	Yarra Valley
FRANCE	Côteaux d'Aix en Provence	
	Côtes de Provence	
	Languedoc-Roussillon	Vins de Pays D'Oc
NEW ZEALAND	North Island	Gisborne, Hawkes Bay, Henderson

MEDIUM

ITALY	Veneto	
AUSTRALIA	Victoria	Yarra Valley
	South Australia	Coonawarra
	Western Australia	Margaret River, Mt Barker
CROATIA	Istria	
SLOVENIA		
ITALY	Umbria, Emilia Romagna	
AUSTRALIA	Southern Australia	Clare, Adelaide Hill, McLaren Vale
USA	Washington	Yakima Valley, Columbia River Basin
ROMANIA	Murfatlar	
USA	California	Monterey
BULGARIA	Plovdiv	
USA	California	Central Napa, Central Sonoma

FULL

BULGARIA	Sukindol, Svishtov, Russe	
CHILE	Maipo, Curico	
SPAIN	Penedés	
SOUTH AFRICA	most regions	
ITALY	Tuscany	
AUSTRALIA	New South Wales	Hunter Valley, Riverina
	South Australia	Barossa Valley
	Western Australia	Swan Valley
USA	California	Northern Napa Valley, Riverside

Make The Grape Connection

Labelled By Grape

AUSTRALIA
BULGARIA
CHILE
CROATIA
FRANCE
Languedoc-Roussillon
(sometimes called Vin de Pays d'Oc)
ITALY
NEW ZEALAND
ROMANIA
SLOVENIA
SOUTH AFRICA
SPAIN
USA

Blended With Other Grapes

In Europe, France in particular, Cabernet Sauvignon is often blended with softer varieties, **but the grape names do not appear on the label**. You may prefer blended wines, so here are some with noticeable Cabernet character with the added complexity of taste that comes with subtle blending. For full information on Bordeaux see BEHIND THE RED BORDEAUX LABEL *(p.149)*.

Country/Region/Labelled As

FRANCE
Bordeaux (claret): Any wine labelled 'Cru Classé' or 'Cru Bourgeois' from the Médoc or Graves districts, particularly St Estèphe, St Julien, Margaux and Pauillac in the Médoc
Côtes de Duras, Côtes Marmandais, Côtes de Fronton, Côtes de Buzet, Bergerac: These are the Bordeaux 'satellites' and, like Bordeaux, the blending wine is Merlot

Côteaux d'Aix en Provence: Ch Vignelaure
Languedoc-Roussillon: Mas de Daumas Gassac
ITALY
Tuscany: 'Tignanello' from Antinori and many other wines from Chianti producers, only allowed to be called Vino da Tavola and usually blended with Sangiovese
SPAIN
Ribera del Duero: Vega Sicilia, Valbuena
PORTUGAL
Setubal: Quinta da Bacolhôa
LEBANON
Bekaa Valley: Ch Musar (blended with Syrah)
AUSTRALIA & NEW ZEALAND
Wines labelled 'Cabernet Shiraz' or 'Cabernet Merlot'
NB: Cabernet is predominant when named first.
USA
California: Dominus, Opus One and wines labelled 'Cabernet Merlot'

PLAYING THE GAME

Some Like it Hot

In each of the following comparisons, the light wines come from cooler areas than the full.

Game One
Cabernet Sauvignon

 *Light*   *Full*

New Zealand
South Island, Marlborough

or

France
Languedoc-Roussillon
(Vins de Pays d'Oc)

V

Australia
New South Wales or
South Australia

or

Bulgaria
Svishtov, Suhindol or Russe

 A–B   Select a full Australian wine 12.5° alcohol +
European wines 3 years, Australia and New Zealand 2 years

Game Two
Cabernet Sauvignon

The choice is large – so here are some 'starters for six'.

Medium

Italy
Veneto
or
Spain
Penedés
or
Australia
Western Australia, Mount Barker

Full

Bulgaria
Plovdiv
or
Australia
New South Wales, Hunter Valley
or
USA
California, Napa Valley

v

A–C Choose medium wines from 12° to 12.5°; full wines from 13° upwards, European wines 4 years, Australia 3 years

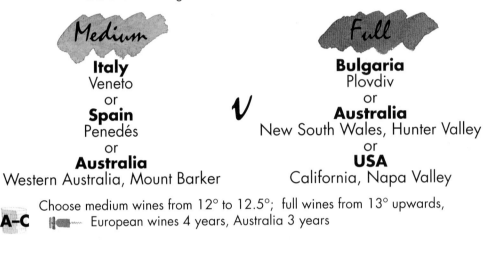

Game Three

Cabernet Sauvignon's reputation stems from Bordeaux where it is always blended; the practice is spreading. Blending usually gives a wine more subtlety. Do you agree?

100%
Cabernet Sauvignon

Australia
Yarra Valley or Coonawarra

or

South Africa
Paarl, Stellenbosch

Blended

Haut Médoc
Pauillac, Bordeaux (Cabernet Sauvignon predominant + Merlot)
or
Lebanon
Ch Musar
(Cabernet Sauvignon predominant + Syrah)
or
Australia
Cabernet-Shiraz
(Cabernet Sauvignon predominant + Shiraz)

v

B–C 4 years France & Lebanon, 3 years Australia & South Africa

WHAT'S ON THE SHELVES

LIGHT

COUNTRY	COMMENTS		
AUSTRALIA			
Victoria	Excellent varietal character. Oak-aged.	**90, 88**	**B–D**
Yarra Valley	Ripe blackcurrant fruit and pronounced cassis smell.	**87, 86**	
	2 to 6 years		
FRANCE			
Provence	Only 10-15% is made as single variety.	**90, 89**	**A–D**
Coteaux d'Aix en Provence	Best come from Provence and Coteaux d'Aix. Good varietal character with some		
Languedoc-Roussillon	blackcurrant fruit.		
	2 to 4 years		
ITALY			
Friuli-Venezia-Giulia	The best have real style and character, more tannin to keep longer.	**90, 89**	**A–B**
	3 to 6 years		
Trentino Alto-Adige	Easy to drink. Soft, rounded fruit.		
	2 to 4 years		
NEW ZEALAND			
South Island	Pale in colour. Oak-aged.	**91, 90**	**B–C**
Marlborough	Grassy herbaceous flavour.	**89, 88**	
	2 to 4 years		
North Island	The warmer climate produces fuller wines.	**90, 89**	**B–C**
Auckland	Oak-aged. Herby spicy flavour. Good balance.		
Gisborne	2 to 5 years. The more expensive		
Hawkes Bay	up to 8		
Henderson			

CABERNET SAUVIGNON – WORLDWIDE

COUNTRY	COMMENTS		
AUSTRALIA			
South Australia Coonawarra	Excellent varietal character. Oak-aged. Pronounced cassis smell. Ripe blackcurrant fruit. 2 to 6 years	90, 88 87, 86 85	B–D
South Australia **Adelaide Hills** **Clare**	More body but still elegant. Rich blackcurrant flavours. 3 to 6 years	90, 88 87, 86	B–D
Western Australia **Margaret River** **Mount Barker**	Bordeaux elegance and style. Oak-aged. Blackcurrant fruit. 3 to 6 years	90, 89 87, 86	B–D
BULGARIA **Plovdiv**	Full colour, powerful smell and taste. Oak-aged. Ripe blackcurrant fruit and tannin. 3 to 6 years		A
CROATIA **Istria Peninsular**	Least typical of European Cabernets, lacking elegance and varietal character. Best from Istria. Oak-aged. Fruity, sometimes too soft. 2 to 5 years		A
ITALY **Emilia Romagna** **Oltrepo, Pavese** **Umbria, Veneto**	Oak-aged. Round, fruity. 3 to 5 years	90, 89 87	A–C
ROMANIA **Murfatlar**	Quality will improve as western markets open up. Oak-aged. Round, rich, almost sweet, tannic. 3 to 8 years	90, 87 86, 84	A
SLOVENIA	As for Croatia above.		
USA **California** **Monterey** **Southern & Central** **Napa Valley** **Southern & Central** **Sonoma**	Stylish elegant wines, deceptively Bordeaux in flavour, representing a recent trend towards lighter, more elegant wines. Lovely cedarwood fruit and backbone. 3 to 8 years. Need bottle-ageing	90, 89 87, 86 85	B–D

FULL

COUNTRY	COMMENTS		
AUSTRALIA			
New South Wales	Deep coloured, rich, powerful wines.	90, 88	A–D
Hunter Valley	A combination of ripe fruit and soft tannin.	87, 86	
Riverina	Concentrated smell and taste of blackcurrants,		
South Australia	sometimes minty eucalyptus.		
Barossa Valley	⊩⊏▦⏦ 3 to 8 years. Needs some bottle-ageing		
Western Australia			
Swan Valley			
BULGARIA			
Russe	Wines with sound varietal character but		A–B
Suhindol	lacking elegance. Oak-aged. Good value.		
Svishtov	Blackcurrant fruit.		
	⊩⊏▦⏦ 2 to 5 years		
CHILE			
Curico	Good varietal flavours. May lack elegance.	90, 89	A–B
Maipo	This is a country to watch. Blackcurrant fruit	88	
	sometimes diluted by excessive oak-ageing.		
	Warm earthy finish.		
	⊩⊏▦⏦ 3 to 6 years		
ITALY	The best and most expensive in Italy. Stylish	90, 88	B–D
Tuscany	wines with finesse, backbone and fruit.	87, 86	
	⊩⊏▦⏦ 4 to 8 years		
SOUTH AFRICA			
most regions	Good blackcurrant fruit and acidity.	91, 90	B
	⊩⊏▦⏦ 2 to 6 years	89, 88	
		87, 86	
SPAIN			
Catalonia	Relative newcomer to Spain. Usually aged	90, 89	B–D
Penedés	in American oak giving pronounced vanilla	87, 86	
	smell. Ripe fruit and good tannin.		
	⊩⊏▦⏦ 3 to 6 years		
USA			
California	Full-bodied, alcoholic, heady wines with	90, 89	A–D
Northern Napa Valley	deep colour. Rich almost sweet blackcurrant	87, 86	
Northern Sonoma	fruit on nose and palate. Good tannin	85	
Russian River	balance but may lack acidity.		
San Luis Obispo	⊩⊏▦⏦ 3 to 8 years – or younger if you like		
Santa Barbara	the strength		

RELIABLE PRODUCERS & SHIPPERS

LIGHT

FRANCE
Coteaux des Baux-en-Provence, Coteaux d'Aix en Provence, Côtes de Provence: Ch de Selle, Ch Vignelaure, Commanderie de la Bargemone, Commanderie de Peyrassol, Domaine des Terres Blanches, Domaine de Trevallon,
Languedoc-Roussillon: Ch de Gourgazaud, Domaine St Martin de la Garrigue, Mas de Daumas Gassac, Mas Chichet

ITALY
Trentino Alto-Adige, Friuli-Veneto: Alois Lageder, Bellavista, Ca' del Bosco, Giorgio Grai, La Stoppa, Maculan, Ronco del Ghemiz, Tenuta San Leonardo, Terre Rosse,

NEW ZEALAND
Auckland, Hawkes Bay: Babich, Brookfield, Coopers Creek, Delegats, Kumeu River, Matua Valley, Cooks Longridge, Morton Estate, Nobilo, Selaks, Stonyridge, Te Mata, Villa Maria, Vidal
Marlborough: Cloudy Bay, Corbans, Montana, Stoneleigh, Vavasour

MEDIUM

AUSTRALIA
Balgownie, Bannockburn, Bowen Estate, Brown Brothers, Cape Clairault, Capel Vale Wines, Cape Mentelle, Ch Tahbilk, Coldstream Hills, Coonawarra, Cullens, Delatite, Evans & Tate, Geoff Merill, Kathook Easte, Leeuwin Estate, Lindemans, Mildara, Moss Wood Estate, Petaluma, Redman (Rouge Homme), Taltarni, Thomas Hardy, Vasse Felix, Virgin Hills, Wirra Wirra, Wynns, Yarra Burn, Yarra Yering

BULGARIA
Plovdiv, Sakar Mountain

CROATIA
Alpi Juliani, Istria

ITALY
Tuscany/Umbria: Antinori (Solaia), Castello dei Rampolla (Sammarco), Isole e Olena (Collezione de Marchi), Lungarotti (San Giorgio), Marchese Incisa della Rochetta (Sassicaia), Villa Banfi (Tavernelle), Villa de Capezzana (Ghiaie della Furba)

SPAIN
Jean Leon, Marques de Grinon, Raimat, Torres

USA
Alexander Valley Vineyards, Buena Vista, Carmenet, Caymus, Clos du Val, Dominus, Dunn Vineyards, Flora Springs, Frey Vineyards (Mendocino County), Frog's Leap, Heitz Wine Cellars, Hess Collection, Kenwood Vineyards, Mayacamas, Monticello, Newton Vineyard, Ridge Vineyards, Robert Mondavi, Simi, Stag's Leap Wine Cellars, Sterling Vineyards

FULL

AUSTRALIA
Berri Estates, Brokenwood, Hungerford Hill, Huntingdon Estate, Lake's Folly, Lindemans, Hunter Valley, Orlando, Penfolds, Rosemount Estate, Saltram, Tyrrells

BULGARIA
Suhindol, Svishtov, Russe

CHILE
Concha y Toro, Cousino Macul, Erraruriz Panquehue, Los Vascos, Linderos, Montes, Santa Rita, Torres, Undurraga

SOUTH AFRICA
Meerlust, Rustenberg, Warwick Estate

USA
Beaulieu, Beringer, Ch Montelena, Cuvaison, Duckhorn, Forman Vineyards, Grgich Hills, Inglenook, Joseph Phelps, Robert Mondavi, Shafer Vineyards

MERLOT
WORLDWIDE

FAMOUS REGION: BORDEAUX

KNOW YOUR GRAPE

Wines labelled as Merlot are comparative newcomers to the shelves and are quickly gaining popularity.

South and south-west France produce 80% of the world's Merlot, where it is mostly blended. It is used in varying proportions, in virtually every bottle of red wine from Bordeaux and its neighbouring districts – see BEHIND THE RED BORDEAUX LABEL *(p.149)*.

FLAVOURS

(PLUMS) (MINT) (FRUIT CAKE) (GAME)

Full-bodied with a deep red colour and plummy, fruit-cake flavour. Naturally soft, pleasing, easy-to-drink wines. Wine writers use a host of descriptions which range from plums and fruit cake through to game. Merlot has less noticeable tannin than Cabernet Sauvignon because of its fruitier flavours.

STYLE

LIGHT	MEDIUM	FULL
✗	✔	✔

Soft pleasing wines usually with 1° more alcohol than Cabernet Sauvignon.

WHEN TO DRINK

A plentiful grape because it ripens early, so inexpensive and good value for money. The lighter and cheaper wines from 2 to 4 years. Powerful, expensive wines from 4 to 10 years (the best Bordeaux even longer).

IS IT EVER BLENDED WITH OTHER GRAPES?

Yes. It is a give-and-take affair. Cabernet Sauvignon wines are softened by the addition of Merlot and Merlot wines gain backbone from the more austere Cabernet Sauvignon. The resulting and differing tastes are explored in BEHIND THE RED BORDEAUX LABEL *(p.149)*.

IS IT OAK-AGED?

Merlot responds well to oak-ageing. Only the lightest and cheapest will be matured in tanks.

HOW MUCH WILL IT COST?

A–C

But only a few in **C**.

IS THE GRAPE NAME ON THE LABEL?

100% wines: Yes. Blended: Yes, except in Bordeaux.

KNOW YOUR STYLE

STYLOMETER

MEDIUM

ITALY	**Trentino Alto-Adige**	
	Friuli-Venezia-Giulia	
	Veneto	
	Emilia-Romagna	
AUSTRALIA	**South Australia**	Coonawarra
	Western Australia	Margaret River, Mount Barker
FRANCE	**Languedoc-Roussillon**	(sometimes labelled Vin de Pays d'Oc)
CROATIA	**Istria**	
SLOVENIA		
USA	**Washington State**	
NEW ZEALAND	**North Island**	Hawkes Bay, Auckland
	South Island	Marlborough, Nelson

FULL

HUNGARY	**Villany**	
BULGARIA	**Russe**	
	Stambolovo	
ROMANIA	**Arad**	
	Dealul Mare	
	Focsani	
SOUTH AFRICA	**Franschoek**	
	Paarl	
	Stellenbosch	
USA	**California**	Napa Valley, Santa Barbara
CHILE	**Maule**	
	Curico	

MAKE THE GRAPE CONNECTION

MERLOT

The following countries produce 100% Merlot wines which are **always labelled by the grape**.

AUSTRALIA
BULGARIA
CHILE
CROATIA
FRANCE
HUNGARY
  (sometimes labelled 'Médoc Noir')
ITALY
NEW ZEALAND
ROMANIA
SLOVENIA
SOUTH AFRICA
USA

BLENDED WITH OTHER GRAPES

Once blended with another grape, two systems of labelling come into play.

LABELLED BY GRAPE

AUSTRALIA
FRANCE
  Languedoc-Roussillon
  (also called Vin de Pays d'Oc)
NEW ZEALAND
USA
  California

LABELLED BY REGION

FRANCE
  Bordeaux
  see BEHIND THE RED BORDEAUX LABEL
  (p.149)
SOUTH AFRICA
  Glen Carlou 'Les Trois'
  Overgaauw 'Tria Corda'

PLAYING THE GAME

Some Like it Hot

Game One
Merlot

The Merlot grape is altogether softer, less noticeably tannic and easier to drink when young, than Cabernet Sauvignon. It also achieves higher alcohol levels, so Merlot wines are medium to full in style. You could compare the two styles over a meal. If you do not taste both together, make sure you taste the medium wine first, so as not to swamp your taste buds.

Medium

Vin de Pays d'Oc or
Languedoc-Roussillon
France
or
Italy
Trentino Alto-Adige or Veneto

A–C 3 years

Full

Hungary
Villany
or
USA
California, Santa Barbara

Game Two

Merlot is the main blending grape in Bordeaux, where winemakers maintain that this is its proper role. Compare a typically Merlot predominant wine with 100% Merlot and see if you agree with them.

Blended

St Emilion or **Fronsac**
Bordeaux
or
New Zealand or **Australia**
Merlot-Cabernet

100%

Croatia
Istria
or
USA
Washington State

A–C Europe and USA 3 years. New Zealand and Australia 2 years

WHAT'S ON THE SHELVES

MEDIUM

COUNTRY	COMMENTS		
AUSTRALIA			
South Australia	Light to medium with excellent fruit, good	91, 90	B–D
Coonawarra	acidity and elegance.	88, 87	
Western Australia	2 to 6 years		
Margaret River			
Mount Barker			
CROATIA	Attractive wines from north west bordering		A
Istria	the Adriatic. Oak-ageing is traditional. Fresh		
	with an easy charm and good acidity.		
	2 to 4 years		
FRANCE			
Languedoc-Roussillon	Oak-ageing is standard. Fruity wines,	90, 89	A
	low in tannin. Plum and fruit cake flavour.	88	
	2 to 4 years		
ITALY			
Emilia-Romagna	Best come from Grave del Friuli and Piavi	90, 88	A–B
Friuli-Venezia-Giulia	where oak-ageing is sometimes used.		
Trentino Alto-Adige	Pleasing, soft wines.		
Veneto	Young and fresh		
NEW ZEALAND			
North Island	Temperate climate is ideal for Merlot. Some	91, 90	A–C
Auckland	oak-ageing is usual. Excellent plummy flavour	89, 88	
Hawkes Bay	with good balance of acidity and fruit.	87, 86	
	2 to 6 years		
SLOVENIA	Pleasing wines from the area bordering Italy		A
	Oak-ageing is traditional. Fruity, easy to drink.		
	2 to 4 years		

COUNTRY	COMMENTS		
USA **Washington State**	Merlot flourishes in this northerly state. Solid, sound, fruity wines. ⊢⊏━ 2 to 6 years	90, 89 88, 87	B–D

FULL

BULGARIA **Russe** **Stambolovo**	Full, rich wines, easy and pleasing to drink. Oak-ageing is traditional. Good balance of fruit and acidity. ⊢⊏━ 2 to 4 years		A
CHILE **Curico** **Maule**	Fruity wines with some good tannin. ⊢⊏━ Can be drunk young	91, 90 89	A–B
HUNGARY **Villany**	Very hot summers produce concentrated, deep coloured wines. Full, rich wines. ⊢⊏━ 2 to 4 years		A
ROMANIA **Arad** (Hungarian Border) **Dealul Mare** (east) **Focsani (east)**	Best come from the regions of Dealul Mare and Focsani. Oak-ageing is traditional. Full, rich with natural sweetness which can make them flabby. ⊢⊏━ 2 to 4 years		A
SOUTH AFRICA **Franschoek** **Paarl** **Stellenbosch**	Increasingly used as a single variety. Fruity, plummy, cherries and raspberries. Mineral undertone. ⊢⊏━ 3 to 8 years	91, 90 89, 87 86, 84	B–C
USA **California** **Napa Valley** **Santa Barbara**	Oak-ageing is standard practice. Full and concentrated. ⊢⊏━ 2 to 6 years	90, 89 88	B–D

RELIABLE PRODUCERS & SHIPPERS

 MEDIUM

 FULL

AUSTRALIA
Berri Estates, De Bortoli, Delatite, Hungerford Hill, Tim Knappstein, Mildara

CROATIA
Milion Merlot

FRANCE
Languedoc-Roussillon:
Corbières – Ch Lastour, Ch le Condamine Bertrand, Ch les Ollieux;
Côteaux du Languedoc – Ch de Nizas, Ch de Salles, Ch Pech-Redon, Domaine des Gres-Ricards

HUNGARY
Supermarket own labels

ITALY
Emilia-Romagna: Terre Rosse
Friuli: Collavini, Gravner, Russiz Superiore
Trentino Alto-Adige: Castel Schwanburg, Cavit, Fedrigotti-Foianeghe, Tenuta San Leonardo
Veneto: Maculan, Santa Margherita, Villa dal Ferro, Zonin

NEW ZEALAND
Esk Valley, Kumeu River, Matua Valley, Vidal

USA
Washington State: Arbor Crest, The Hogue Cellars

BULGARIA
Russe, Stambolovo

CHILE
Coliteros, Concha y Toro, Errazus Parqueterre, San Pedro

HUNGARY
Supermarkets/merchants own labels

ROMANIA
Supermarkets/merchants own labels

SOUTH AFRICA
Franschoek: La Motte
Paarl: Glen Carlou
Stellenbosch: Meerlust, Overgaauw

USA
California: Clos du Bois, Clos du Val, Firestone Vineyard, Glen Ellen, Inglenook, Newton Vineyards, Rutherford Hill

BEHIND THE RED BORDEAUX LABEL
CABERNET SAUVIGNON & MERLOT

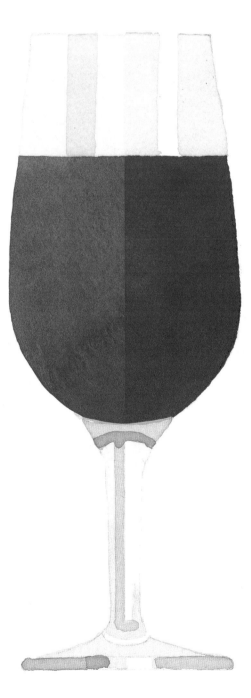

KNOW YOUR GRAPE

Bordeaux is the world's favourite red wine, traditionally called claret in the UK. There are 24,000 growers, who make it the world's largest and most famous Quality wine-producing region. On the face of things, it looks an easy wine to buy; the bottles all look the same and the labels are similar, nearly all saying Château something or other. Everything about red Bordeaux seems to infer a common taste.

In fact there is not one, because 99% of the wines are blended and the blends vary noticeably in different parts of Bordeaux. This guide explains the differing tastes and shows you how to pick the right bottle for your taste.

Any red wine bearing the Bordeaux name on the label can only be made from five specified grapes. Three play the most important role: Cabernet Sauvignon, Cabernet Franc and Merlot. The key to picking the right bottle is firstly to know which predominant grape taste you prefer and in turn which regions they come from, as the label does not disclose the grapes used in the blend. Taste and style vary enormously depending on firstly the grape, then the climate, soil and the skill of the winemaker. Although each region has its own traditions, the blend is ultimately at the discretion of each of the 24,000 growers.

PREDOMINANTLY CABERNET SAUVIGNON

West of the River Gironde
Graves, Médoc

Cabernet Sauvignon thrives on well drained, gravel soil. A low yielding and therefore expensive variety. It also ripens late, so in cold years it is altogether too tough and tannic until it is mature. An expensive pastime. Hence the need for blending with the softer, more generous Merlot.

PREDOMINANTLY MERLOT

East of the River Gironde
St Emilion, Pomerol

Merlot likes heavier soil. A high yielding vine, so cheaper to grow than Cabernet Sauvignon. Its soft, generous character makes it an ideal partner for the austere Cabernet. On its own it can be too bland, so Cabernet is added to give backbone and balance.

FLAVOURS

BLACKCURRANT

Strongly blackcurrant with great depth of flavour. More vegetal when mature, with undertones of cedarwood.

FRUIT CAKE **PLUM**

Soft, generous fruit.

STYLE

Powerful tannic wine, aggressive in youth but maturing into elegant, complex wines.

Lower in tannin than Cabernet Sauvignon but 1% higher in alcohol.

WHEN TO DRINK

Basic Bordeaux from 18 months.

Cabernet Sauvignon: Better wines
from 4 years.
Merlot: Less expensive wines from
3 years.

In good years, with plenty of sunshine
(and there was plenty in the '80s) you can
drink sooner. See VINTAGE GUIDE *(p.160)*
for best wines in bands **C–D**.

ARE THEY EVER UNBLENDED?

Hardly ever.

IS THE GRAPE NAME ON THE LABEL?

Only for a very few of the cheapest wines.

ARE THEY OAK-AGED?

Both respond particularly well to oak-
ageing and all but the cheapest wines
produced in large volume will be aged
in oak.

HOW MUCH WILL THEY COST?
A–D

From the sublime to the ridiculous. From
very low band **A** to four figures under the
auctioneer's hammer.

CABERNET FRANC is the third main variety. It is a more muted version of Cabernet Sauvignon, with softer acids and tannins. Herbaceous, vegetal flavours and aroma. It grows well in the cooler soil east of the River Gironde. A high yielder and early ripener, so less expensive than Cabernet Sauvignon and used extensively in the cheaper wines. It is always blended. With rare exception (Ch Cheval Blanc, St Emilion, the most famous) it is the minor partner in any blend.

KNOW YOUR STYLE

There are 16 major wine regions within the whole of the Bordeaux wine-producing area, some with sub-districts. Here we show the regions where each grape predominates.

CABERNET SAUVIGNON PREDOMINANT

Graves: Pessac-Léognan
Medoc
Haut Medoc: Listrac, Margaux, Moulis, Pauillac, St Estèphe, St Julien

MERLOT PREDOMINANT

Canon-Fronsac
Côtes de Castillon
Côtes de Francs
Pomerol
Lalande de Pomerol
St Emilion
Lussac-St Emilion
Montagne-St Emilion
Puisseguin-St Emilion
St Georges-St Emilion

50/50 (Approx)

Côtes de Bourg
Premières Côtes de Blaye
Fronsac

STYLOMETER

Predominant grape: CS = Cabernet Sauvignon; M = Merlot

LIGHT

50/50	**Bordeaux, Bordeaux Supérieur**
50/50	**Premières Côtes de Bordeaux**

MEDIUM

50/50	**Côtes de Bourg**
50/50	**Premières Côtes de Blaye**
50/50	**Fronsac**
CS	**Médoc**
M	**Côtes de Castillon**
M	**Côtes de Francs**
M	**Lalande de Pomerol**
M	**Canon-Fronsac**

FULL

CS	**Graves**	Pessac-Léognan
CS	**Haut Médoc**	Listrac, Margaux, Moulis, Pauillac, St Estèphe, St Julien
M	**St Emilion, Lussac-St Emilion, Montagne-St Emilion, Puisseguin-St Emilion, St Georges-St Emilion**	
M	**Pomerol**	

MAKE THE GRAPE CONNECTION

APPELLATION CONTROLEE

There are three levels of AC in Bordeaux. The largest covers the whole Bordeaux wine-producing area, then come the regions within the whole area. Finally, the villages or 'communes' within the regions. As the area gets smaller, the wines get more expensive and, in theory, are of a better quality.

VILLAGES
or 'Communes'
(12% of all red Bordeaux)
The most famous are in Haut-Médoc & Graves regions.

REGIONS
(38% of all red Bordeaux wines)

BORDEAUX
The whole area (50%)

CLASSIFICATIONS OR CRUS CLASSES

Within the regions or villages there are individual estates or châteaux. Over the years, an order of merit or system of classification has evolved. Out of 4,000 or so châteaux, a mere 289 – mainly from the Médoc, Graves and St Emilion regions – have been singled out. It is not surprising that they command the highest prices. The number of classified châteaux in each region or village is shown in brackets.

The classifications are a broad guide only to quality, for there are many fine châteaux which remain unclassified, most notably in Pomerol. **The classifications almost always appear on the label**.

REGION/CLASSIFICATIONS

CABERNET SAUVIGNON PREDOMINANT

MEDOC/Grand Cru Classé (61)
Divided into five groups, number one ranked top and most expensive. Contains the famous Châteaux Margaux, Lafite, Latour & Mouton-Rothschild
MEDOC/Crus Bourgeois (141)
The second division

GRAVES/Grands Crus Classé (13)
There are very few classified Graves but they include the top-rated Ch Haut-Brion, ranked with the first tier of Médoc Grands Crus.

MERLOT PREDOMINANT
ST EMILION/Premiers Grands Crus Classé (11)
This category contains the great Ch Cheval Blanc and Ch Ausone
ST EMILION/Grands Crus Classé (63)

CABERNET SAUVIGNON PREDOMINANT

If you like the taste of Cabernet Sauvignon, you will probably enjoy wines from the following regions and villages:

LABELLED AS	AVERAGE %
MEDOC	60%
GRAVES	70%
HAUT MEDOC	60–70%
Listrac	70%
Moulis	70%
Margaux	75%
Pauillac	75%
St Estèphe	75%
St Julien	75%

MERLOT PREDOMINANT

If you like the taste of Merlot, you will probably enjoy wines from the following districts:

LABELLED AS	AVERAGE %
FRONSAC	50%
COTES DE BOURG	50%
PREMIERES COTES DE BLAYE	50%
ST EMILION	60%
LUSSAC-ST EMILION	60%
PUISSEGUIN-ST EMILION	60%
MONTAGNE-ST EMILION	60%
ST GEORGES-ST EMILION	60%
COTES DE CASTILLON	60%
COTES DE FRANCS	60%
LALANDE DE POMEROL	60%
CANON FRONSAC	65%
POMEROL	80%

NB: The percentages shown are a broad guide only. They may change significantly if either the Cabernet or Merlot crop fails. For example, the Merlot crop was totally decimated by frost in 1984 and so most wines had a higher than usual percentage of Cabernet, although it is more often the winemaker who is the final arbiter of the blend and the variations are enormous.

PLAYING THE GAME

Game One
Which Grape?

Although invariably blended, most Bordeaux red wines are either Cabernet Sauvignon or Merlot predominant so, most importantly, which taste do you prefer? The following two wines are chosen to show the most obvious difference. Each has the highest average percentage of either Cabernet Sauvignon or Merlot in their respective regions.

Cabernet Sauvignon Predominant   *v*   ### Merlot Predominant

Pauillac   **Pomerol**

A–B   From 4 years
Choose wines in the same price band

Game Two
Which Commune or Region?

As we have shown, there are several regions either side of the river whose wines have approximately the same percentage of Cabernet and Merlot but different micro-climates. Variations in the soil and the aspect of the vineyards produce different styles and flavours. The following comparisons are designed to show the regional differences.

Cabernet Sauvignon Predominant
(Average 70%)

Listrac or **Moulis**   *v*   **Graves**

or (Average 75%)

St Julien or **Margaux**   *v*   **Pauillac** or **St Estèphe**

Merlot Predominant
(Average 60%)

St Emilion   *v*   **Lalande de Pomerol**

A–C   4 years upwards
Choose wines of approximately the same price

155

Game Three
Which Year?

Vintages in Bordeaux are very important. The vintage notes on p.160 show how each year produces a different style of wine. The 1980s produced a remarkable run of good years. Happily, there are two sets of consecutive years which give a fascinating example of how style varies from one year to another. Choose wines from the same region, or, for perfect comparison, from the same Château and of the same approximate price.

1982   *V*   1983

You will notice how the 1982 – product of an exceptionally hot year – is much softer and richer than the more tannic 1983, again grown in a good year but with a more typical balance of rain and sun through the growing season.

1985   *V*   1986

The wines of 1985 were from another very good year (not quite so hot as 1982) and made rich, but not opulent, powerful wines which create an interesting comparison with the lighter but beautifully balanced wines of 1986.

WHAT'S ON THE SHELVES

The weather plays a vital role in Bordeaux in shaping the style of the wines, so vintages are all-important. For a general guide to the style and character of recent vintages see p.160. (NB: Grape column shows predominant grape: M = Merlot CS = Cabernet Sauvignon)

LIGHT

REGION	GRAPE	COMMENTS	
BORDEAUX **BORDEAUX SUPERIEUR** **PREMIERES COTES DE BORDEAUX** (sometimes with château name)	M	Plummy. 18 months after the vintage	**A**

MEDIUM

CANON-FRONSAC	M	An up-and-coming region. Soft, plummy Merlot characteristics. 3 to 6 years	**A–B**
COTES DE BOURG	50/50	Good, sound wines, excellent value. More blackcurrant than ordinary Bordeaux. 3 to 10 years for the best	**A–B**
COTES DE CASTILLON	M	Easy-to-drink wines. Plummy, fruity. Delicious from 2 to 4 years	**A**
COTES DE FRANCS	M	Similar to Côtes de Castillon. 2 to 4 years	**A**

157

REGION	GRAPE	COMMENTS	
FRONSAC	M	Soft, plummy, fruitcake. 3 to 6 years	A–B
LALANDE DE POMEROL	M	Rich, plummy wines. 3 to 7 years	B
MEDOC	CS	The source for much of the Cabernet predominant, archetypal red Bordeaux. Blackcurrant fruit and tannin. 3 to 5 years	A–B
PREMIERES COTES DE BLAYE	50/50	Sometimes with more Merlot than Côtes de Bourg, so softer and more plummy. 3 to 5 years	A–B

FULL

REGION	GRAPE	COMMENTS	
GRAVES Pessac-Léognan	CS	Powerful, tannic wines, hints of blackcurrant drier and more austere than Haut-Médoc with an earthy taste. 4 to 10 years. Red Graves often have a flat period in years 5 and 6 but fully recover to give complex flavours	B–D
HAUT-MEDOC Listrac	CS	Powerful, rich blackcurrant, sometimes a bit austere; good value. 4 to 10 years	B–C
Margaux	CS	Perfumed bouquet, great charm and finesse. Rich blackcurrant, very pure and complex when aged. 4 to 10 years, more for best wines	B–D
Moulis	CS	As for Listrac. As for Listrac	B–C

REGION	GRAPE	COMMENTS	
HAUT-MEDOC			
Pauillac	CS	Most powerful and concentrated of Médoc villages. Intense blackcurrant fruit, high tannin. Develop into beautiful, complex wines.	**B–D**
		5 to 10 years and well beyond for finest wines in great years	
St Estèphe	CS	Full blackcurrant, deep colour, high in tannin so sometimes rather severe.	**B–D**
		5 to 10 years and often well beyond	
St Julien	CS	The most attractive of Médoc village wines. Lovely bouquet and flavour of blackcurrant, more finesse and delicacy than Pauillac.	**B–D**
		5 to 10 years + for the top crus	
POMEROL	M	The smallest of the village areas. Rich, plummy, full wines with noticeable tannin to give almost Médoc style when young. Opulent and complex with age.	**B–D**
		5 to 10 years + for best wines in bands	**C–D**
ST EMILION	M	Soft, quite low in tannin, plummy fruit.	**B–D**
		3 years for inexpensive wines, from 4 to 10 for the best	
ST EMILION Lussac-, Montagne-, Puisseguin- & St Georges-St Emilion	M	Often better than inexpensive straightforward St Emilion. Flavour as St Emilion, but lighter in style.	**B–C**
		3 to 8 years	

BEHIND THE RED BORDEAUX LABEL CABERNET SAUVIGNON & MERLOT

VINTAGES

The date on a bottle of wine refers to the year in which the grapes were grown and picked. In Bordeaux, it is a vital clue to the taste, which is dependent on the variable weather.

1980
Awful, early summer with decent August and September. So small vintage of generally poor quality. Light and usually characterless wines. If you have any bottles, drink them now.

1981
Very good weather, until rains at vintage time. So variable year with Cabernet more successful than Merlot. Drink St Emilion and Crus Bourgeois now. Médocs and Graves can be kept another two or three years.

1982
Untypically hot year. Almost a 'New World' vintage. Wines very rich, soft and flattering. Best are superb and need keeping. Both Cabernet and Merlot produced wonderful wines. Many St Emilions and other Merlot dominant wines are already lovely to drink but, like Cabernets of the Médoc and Graves, will last for ever. For wines in **B–D**, this is a vintage to keep and savour.

1983
Right mixture of rain and sun produced classic Bordeaux vintage: sugar, tannin and acidity in perfect balance without opulence of the '82s. Both Cabernet and Merlot can be patchy in quality but start drinking Crus Bourgeois and lesser wines now. Keep the better Médocs and Graves until the mid '90s.

1984
Shocking weather destroyed the Merlot crop, so small yields in St Emilion, Pomerol and other Merlot dominant districts east of Gironde. Generally, wines are expensive, thin and untypical. Not a vintage to select.

1985
Very decent spring and summer followed by a marvellous September produced enormous vintage in volume and better than average wines. Half way between the '82 and '83 in style, a bit richer than usual but not so opulent as the '82. Drink Crus Bourgeois and lesser wines now if you must. They will continue to improve.

1986
Another excellent growing season producing the largest volume of wine in Bordeaux history. Definitely a Cabernet year, so Médoc and Graves will shine. Too early yet to make final judgements but the wines are very well balanced with deep colour, fruit and tannin. Not as big or powerful as the '85s. Drink the main regional basics, i.e. Bordeaux or Bordeaux Superieur and band **A** now. Worth waiting a year or so for band **C** wine.

1987
Another very large but rain-affected vintage producing wines low in tannin and acidity. They will mature early. Drink lesser wines now but do not expect too much. Light and pleasant drinking.

1988
Potentially very great year, with ripe rich wines from St Emilion and Pomerol. Good, classically elegant wines from Graves and Pessac-Léognan, with a mixed bag from the Médoc. Drink lesser wines from 1992, wait for the better wines until 1995 onwards.

1989

Earliest harvest of the century, but with wines that lacked some necessary acidity. Very rich wines, best in the Médoc (with Cabernet Sauvignon), sometimes too ripe in St Emilion/ Pomerol (where Merlot predominates). Start drinking the lesser wines in 1993–1994.

1990

Wines that are high in alcohol and tannins, suggesting they will be long-lived. Cabernet Sauvignon wines are very ripe. Drink lesser wines from 1995–1996 onwards.

1991

After a series of great years, this is a lesser vintage but useful quantity.

These are general guidelines only. Good winemakers make good, even excellent wines in average and poor years. Whereas bad winemakers can make a mess of things even in good years.

Bordeaux is a vast subject and it is the purpose of these guides to concentrate on the practical side of choosing wines that will suit you. For those who would like to study in more depth, we give a list of recommended books on p.216.

RELIABLE PRODUCERS & SHIPPERS

The range of wines from Bordeaux in most shops is greater than from any other wine region. This selection of Châteaux currently produces fine wines at reasonable prices for their quality and all are widely available.

THE MAIN REGION
Bordeaux:
Châteaux – Beau-Rivage, Chevalier de Vedrines, de Brondeau, du Juge, la Dominique Siegla, Lalande, la Tour Mirabeau, Maître d'Estournel, Méaume, Sables-Peytraud, Selection Jean-Pierre Moueix, Senailhac, Sirius, Thieuley, Timberlay, many merchants' and supermarket own label Clarets

THE REGIONS
Côtes de Bourg/Blaye:
Châteaux – Cap- Martin, de Barbe, du Bousquet, Fontblanche, Guionne, Haut-Sociando, la Croix de Millorit, Lalibarde, L'Escadre, les Moines, Mendoce, Mille-Sescousses, Peyraud, Segonzac
Côtes de Castillon/Côtes de Francs:
Châteaux – de Belcier, du Palanquey, la Clotte, Montbadon, Moulin Rouge, Pitray, Puygueraud
Fronsac/Canon Fronsac:
Châteaux – Cannon de Brem, Coustolle, de la Dauphine, Jeandeman, la Rivière, La Valade, Mayne Vieil, Mazeris, Moulin-Haut-Laroque, Pichelèbre
Graves:
Châteaux – Cabannieux, Chantegrive, Chicane, Coucheroy, de Roquetaillade-La-Grange, la Garde, la Louvière, Rahoul
Médoc/Haut Médoc:
Châteaux – Barreyres, Beaumont, Bel-Orme-Tronquoy-de-Lalande, Blaignan, Cantemerle, Caronne-Ste-Gemme, Cissac, Citran, Coufran, du Castéra, Greysac, Hanteillan, la Cardonne, la Claire, la Tonnelle, la Tour de By, La Tour-St Bonnet, Lanesson, Larose-Trintaudon, les Ormes-Sorbet, Liversan, Loudenne, Malescasse, Patache d'Aux, Pomys, Potensac, Ramage la Batisse, Roquegrave, St Bonnet, Sénéjac, Villegorge
Pomerol/Lalande de Pomerol:
Châteaux – Beauregard, Belles-Graves, Clinet, Clos René, des Annereaux, Evangile, Gazin, La Conseillante, Lafleur-Gazin, Latour-à-Pomerol, le Bon Pasteur, l'Eglise-Clinet, L'Enclos, les Hautes Tuileries, Moulinet, Nenin, Petit-Village, Plince, Siaurac, Trotanoy, Vieux Certan

Premières Côtes de Bordeaux:
Châteaux – Bel-Air-Montaigne, Lafitte (sic), Laroche, Le Gardera, Peyrat, Reynon
St Emilion and Satellites:
Châteaux – Balestard-la-Tonnelle, Belair-Montaiguillon, Cadet-Piola, Croque-Michotte, de Ferrand, Fombrauge, Fonplégade, Fonroque, Franc-Mayne, Haut-Bernat, la Dominique, Larmande, Laroque, l'Arrosée, la Serre, la Tour-du-Pin-Figeac, le Tertre-Rôteboeuf, Maison-Blanche, Monbousquet, Vieux-Ch-Guibeau

THE VILLAGES
GRAVES
Pessac-Léognan
Châteaux – Bouscaut, Carbonnieux, de Fieuzal, de France, la Louvière, Haut-Bailly, Olivier
HAUT MEDOC
Margaux
Châteaux – d'Angludet, d'Issan, du Tertre, Kirwan, la Gurgue, Labégorce-Zédé, La Tour-de-Mons, Monbrison, Prieuré-Lichine, Rausan-Ségla, Siran
Moulis/Listrac
Châteaux – Chasse-Spleen, Clarke, Duplessis-Fabre, Dutruch-Grand-Poujeaux, Fonréaud, Fourcas-Dupré, Fourcas-Hosten, Maucaillou, Poujeaux
Pauillac
Châteaux – Clerc-Milon, Colombier-Monpelou, Fonbadet, Grand-Puy-Lacoste, Haut-Bages-Libéral, Haut-Batailley, Pédesclaux, Pontet-Canet
St Estèphe
Châteaux – Beau-Site, Calon-Ségur, de Pez, Haut Marbuzet, Cos Labory, Lafon-Rochet, Meyney, les Ormes-de-Pez, Phélan-Ségur, Tronquoy-Lalande
St Julien
Châteaux – Beychevelle, Branaire-Ducru, Du Glana, Gloria, Lagrange, Langoa-Barton, Léoville-Barton, St Pierre, Talbot, Terrey-Gros-Caillou

SYRAH
WORLDWIDE

FAMOUS REGION: RHONE VALLEY

KNOW YOUR GRAPE

Syrah, although one of the world's most renowned grapes, is not yet widely planted outside France except in Australia where, known as Shiraz, it is the major red grape.

As one might expect from a grape originating in Iran, the Syrah flourishes in warm regions.

So, it is not surprising that the French, observing the success of Australian Shiraz, are now producing 100% Syrah wines – clearly labelled by grape name – in the Languedoc-Roussillon region. No doubt South Africa and the USA will also begin to give this grape more attention.

FLAVOURS

BLACKCURRANT · SPICE · PEPPER · MINT · EUCALYPTUS

STYLE

LIGHT ✗ MEDIUM ✓ FULL ✓

Usually medium to full-bodied, dry but rich. High tannin and deep colour. Big, full-bodied wines with alcoholic strength of 13° or over. Powerful stuff!

WHEN TO DRINK

Too big and tannic to drink very young, so start from 3 years.

IS IT EVER BLENDED WITH OTHER GRAPES?

Yes, in France to boost other varieties such as Grenache which alone often lacks backbone. In Australia it is regularly blended with Cabernet Sauvignon.

IS IT OAK-AGED

Syrah, like all classic red grapes, responds to oak-ageing. In the northern Rhône in France, the best wines are always fermented in oak.

IS THE GRAPE NAME ON THE LABEL?

Yes, except in the Rhône Valley, France.

HOW MUCH WILL IT COST?

A–D

KNOW YOUR STYLE

STYLOMETER

MEDIUM

FRANCE	**Vins de Pays d'Oc**
	Ardèche
SOUTH AFRICA	**Stellenbosch**
	Paarl
AUSTRALIA	**South Australia** Coonawarra
	Victoria Yarra Valley
	Western Australia Mount Barker

FULL

FRANCE	**Northern Rhône** see DOWN THE RHONE VALLEY *(p.179)*
AUSTRALIA	**New South Wales** Hunter Valley
	South Australia Barossa Valley, McLaren Vale, Coonawarra
USA	**California** Napa Valley, Monterey, Santa Barbara

MAKE THE GRAPE CONNECTION

100% SYRAH

LABELLED BY GRAPE

FRANCE
Ardèche
Languedoc-Roussillon
(Various Vins de Pays)
AUSTRALIA
as Shiraz
SOUTH AFRICA
as Shiraz
USA
California

LABELLED BY REGION

FRANCE
Northern Rhône – see DOWN THE
RHONE VALLEY *(p.179)*

BLENDED

LABELLED BY GRAPE

AUSTRALIA
The predominant grape named first

LABELLED BY REGION

FRANCE
Provence
Southern Rhône – see DOWN THE RHONE
VALLEY *(p.179)*

HERMITAGE
APPELLATION HERMITAGE CONTROLÉE
Domaine des Remizières
DESMEURE P.

DOMAINE SAINT GAYAN

Côtes-du-Rhône

GOLD MEDAL	1987	HOBART	CLASS 54
GOLD MEDAL	1987	MELBOURNE	CLASS 69
GOLD MEDAL	1985	HOBART	CLASS 22

75cl

Rouge Homme
1985
COONAWARRA
SHIRAZ CABERNET

750 ml
alc. 12.5% vol.
PRODUCED AND BOTTLED BY ROUGE HOMME WINES PTY LTD, COONAWARRA, S.A. AUSTRALIA

PLAYING THE GAME

France or Australia

A pure, 100% Syrah (Shiraz in Australia) makes big, powerful wines which, when used for blending, add enormous weight.

So these tastings are more suited to autumnal or winter days.

Game One
Syrah or Shiraz Predominant

Start by discovering whether you prefer the style of Syrah in France or as Shiraz in Australia.

Syrah

Ardèche
Rhône Valley, France
or
Crozes Hermitage
Northern Rhône, France

Shiraz

Australia
Coonawarra or Barossa Valley, South Australia, or
Mount Barker, Western Australia or Hunter Valley, NSW

A–B France 4 years, Australia 3 years

Game Two
Blended

If you find Syrah/Shiraz too powerful on its own, compare wines which have Syrah in the blend but not as the predominant variety. From France, you will find these in either the Southern Rhône, or in most wines from the great sweep of vineyards inland from the Mediterranean: Languedoc-Roussillon and Corbières.

Côtes du Rhône or
Côtes du Roussillon
France
The blends contain Grenache, Cinsaut and Mourvèdre, and sometimes Carignan

Australia
Cabernet-Shiraz
The first named grape is always predominant

A–C as above

WHAT'S ON THE SHELVES

SYRAH (SHIRAZ) PREDOMINANT

COUNTRY	COMMENTS		

AUSTRALIA
New South Wales
  Hunter Valley
South Australia
  Barossa Valley
  Coonawarra
  McLaren Vale
Victoria
  Yarra Valley
Western Australia
  Mount Barker
	Syrah, known as Shiraz, is the most widely planted red grape in Australia. Ranges from the lighter, easy-to-drink, fruity wines to the gutsy, spicy wines with tannin and a concentration of taste. Flavours of rich blackcurrant, mint and eucalyptus with soft tannins. A lighter, drier, more peppery Rhône-like style is made in cooler regions of Coonawarra, Victoria and Western Australia.
	 3 to 8 years
		91, 90
		88, 87
		86, 85
			A–D

FRANCE **Ardèche**	Good varietal character, lighter than Northern Rhône wines. Spicy, fruity. 3 to 5 years	**90, 89** **88**	**A–B**
Languedoc-Roussillon	Increasingly used as a single varietal in the many Vin de Pays of southern France. Light, dry, peppery fruit. 3 to 5 years	**90, 89**	**A–B**
Northern Rhône	See DOWN THE RHONE VALLEY (p.179).		
SOUTH AFRICA **Paarl** **Stellenbosch**	Some wines are on the light side and a little bitter. Best are smoky and spicy. 3 to 8 years	**90, 89** **88, 87**	**B**

COUNTRY	COMMENTS		
USA			
California	Concentrated peppery, blackcurrant	90, 89	B
Napa Valley	flavours with good tannin balance.	87, 86	
Monterey	▮▭ 3 to 8 years		
Santa Barbara			

BLENDED WINES

AUSTRALIA			
New South Wales	Sometimes blended with Cabernet Sauvignon	91, 90	A–D
Hunter Valley	Full-bodied, combining spicy, peppery,	88, 87	
South Australia	minty flavours of Shiraz with the riper	86	
Barossa Valley	blackcurrant fruit of Cabernet Sauvignon.		
McLaren Vale	▮▭ 3 to 8 years		

FRANCE			
Languedoc-Roussillon	Syrah adds flavour of herbs and spices.	90, 89	A
Corbières	Seldom predominant and used to add	88	
Costières de Nîmes	backbone.		
Coteaux du Languedoc	▮▭ 3 to 5 years		
Côtes du Roussillon			
Fitou			
Minervois			
Northern Rhône	See DOWN THE RHONE VALLEY (p.179).		
Provence	Used to improve flavour, quality and style	90, 89	A–C
Aix-en-Provence	of the more traditional Carignon, Cinsaut		
Côtes de Provence	and Grenache based wines. Syrah adds		
	spice, body and backbone. Particularly		
	successful blended with Cabernet Sauvignon.		
	▮▭ 3 to 5 years		
Southern Rhône	See DOWN THE RHONE VALLEY (p.179).		

RELIABLE PRODUCERS & SHIPPERS

AUSTRALIA
Berri Estates, Bowen Estate, Brown Brothers, Ch Tahbilk, Henschke, Hill-Smith Estate, Lindemans, McWilliams, Mitchell, Orlando, Penfolds, Peterson, Rosemount Estate, Rothbury Estate, Saltram, Seppelt, Taltarni, Thomas Hardy, Tim Adams, Tyrrells, Wynns

FRANCE
Ardèche
Louis Latour
Languedoc-Roussillon
Corbières: Ch de Cabrane, Ch les Ollirux, Ch St Auriol, Domaine de Fontsainte, Domaine de Reverend
Coteaux du Languedoc: Ch Rouquette-sur-Mer, Domaine de l'Abbaye Valfernière
Fitou: Caves de Mont-Tauch, Chantovent, Mme Claude Parmentier, Terre Natale
Minervois: Ch de Ollieux, Ch les Palais, Ch le Lastours

Northern Rhône
see DOWN THE RHONE VALLEY *(p.179)*
Provence
Côtes de Provence: Ch Minuty, Commanderie de Peyrassol, Domaine des Hauts de St Jean, Domaine du St Esprit, Domaine Richeaume, La Bernarde, Les Maîtres Vigerons de la Presqu'île de St Tropez, L'Estandon, St André de Figuière,
Coteaux d'Aix en Provence: Ch de Beaulieu, Ch de Fonscolombe, Ch la Gaude, Commanderie de la Bargemone, Domaines les Bastides, Marquis de Saporta
Southern Rhône
see DOWN THE RHONE VALLEY *(p.179)*

USA
California
Bonny Doon, Joseph Phelps, McDowell Valley

GRENACHE
WORLDWIDE

FAMOUS REGIONS: SOUTHERN RHONE, FRANCE
RIOJA, SPAIN

KNOW YOUR GRAPE

Grenache originated in Spain where it is known as Garnacha. It is nearly always blended. This does not make Grenache less important. The current fashion for single variety wines has diverted attention from the great blended wines of the world. Every cook knows that some of the best flavours come from the subtle blending of various ingredients, and so it is with wine.

Grenache acts as the skeleton, supplying the backbone for the blending grapes, which can be compared to the flesh and muscle. The naturally pale colour of this grape also makes it suitable for vin rosé. One of the world's best is Tavel Rosé which has a high proportion of Grenache in the blend.

FLAVOURS

MIXED SOFT RED FRUITS

Soft and sweetish. The final taste mainly comes from the differing grape varieties used in the blending process. See WHAT'S ON THE SHELVES for individual tastes *(p.177)*.

STYLE

LIGHT	MEDIUM	FULL
✘	✔	✔

High in alcohol, pale colour. Low in tannin, so frequently used to soften high tannin wines such as Syrah and Cabernet. The style depends on the varieties with which it is blended and in what proportion.

IS THE GRAPE NAME ON THE LABEL?

Only rarely in Spain, with the synonym Garnacha.

IS IT OAK-AGED?

Yes, nearly always in Rioja and parts of Southern Rhône. Grenache benefits from some ageing in oak.

WHEN TO DRINK

Vins de Pays from 2 to 3 years. Others from 3 years.

HOW MUCH WILL IT COST?

A–D

IS IT EVER UNBLENDED?

Very seldom.

KNOW YOUR STYLE

STYLOMETER

The style of each wine, even from the same region, will vary depending on the percentage of the other grapes which the individual winemaker chooses to blend with Grenache. The alcoholic strength, shown on the label, gives an indication of the style, i.e. under 12° for light, 12° to 13° for medium, over 13° for full.

MEDIUM

FRANCE	**Southern Rhône**	see DOWN THE RHONE VALLEY *(p.179)*
	Côtes de Provence (also rosé)	
	Coteaux d'Aix en Provence (also rosé)	
	Côtes de Luberon	
	Tavel	(rosé only)
	Lirac	(also rosé)
	Languedoc-Roussillon	
SPAIN	**Rioja**	(also rosado)
	Navarra	(also rosado)

FULL

FRANCE	**Southern Rhône**	see DOWN THE RHONE VALLEY *(p.179)*
ITALY	**Sardinia**	
SPAIN	**Ribera del Duero**	
	Rioja Gran Reserva	

MAKE THE GRAPE CONNECTION

100% GRENACHE

LABELLED BY GRAPE

SPAIN
Navarra, labelled as Garnacha

LABELLED BY REGION

ITALY
Cannonau, Sardinia

BLENDED

The southern vineyards of France are beginning to put the grape names on the labels. Where there is still no mention, you can be pretty sure that Grenache plays an important part in the blend.

FRANCE
Costières de Nimes
Côte de Provence
Coteaux d'Aix en Provence
Côtes de Luberon
Languedoc-Roussillon
Lirac
Southern Rhône – see DOWN THE RHONE VALLEY *(p.179)*
Tavel (rosé)

SPAIN
Alicante
Cataluña
Navarra
Ribera del Duero
Rioja

PLAYING THE GAME

Grenache Predominant

The two countries which use Grenache (Garnacha) widely as a blending wine are France and Spain. In France with a selection of varieties and in Spain with the native Tempranillo grape.

Game One
France v Spain

France   *Medium*   *Spain*

Côte du Rhône Villages   ✓   **Basic Rioja**
Southern Rhône

A–B 3 years

Full
✓

Gigondas   **Rioja Gran Reserva**
Southern Rhône

B–C 4 years+

Game Two
Regional (all Medium)

If you prefer one country's taste to another, then it is interesting to make regional comparisons. You could start with the following selections:-

France

Vacqueyras	V	**Minervois**
Southern Rhône		Languedoc-Roussillon

 A-B   3 years

or Spain

Basic Rioja	V	**Navarra**

 A-B   3 years

Game Three
Rosé (Rosado in Spain)

Rosés are very under-rated and good ones make delicious wines for summer drinking. We find the Spanish rosés more earthy.

Tavel	V	**Spain**
Southern Rhône, France		Rioja or Navarra

 A-C   3 years

Side margin: **GRENACHE – WORLDWIDE**

What's On The Shelves

Red Wines

COUNTRY	COMMENTS		
FRANCE			
Languedoc-Roussillon	Virtually every area of Mediterranean vineyards from Montpellier to the Spanish border uses Grenache in its wines. Fitou, Maury and Minervois have the highest percentages. Soft ripe flavours with relatively high alcohol and low acidity.	90, 89	A
	⌇ 2 to 3 years		
Provence	Herbal flavours. In Coteaux d'Aix en Provence	90, 89	A–C
Coteaux d'Aix en Provence	Cabernet Sauvignon adds bite and a flavour of blackcurrants.		
Côtes de Provence	⌇ 3 to 6 years		
Côtes du Luberon			
Southern Rhône	See Down the Rhone Valley (p.179).		
ITALY			
Sardinia	Full-bodied, heady wines with a minimum of 13.5° alcohol.	90, 88	A–B
	⌇ 3 to 5 years		
SPAIN			
Alicante	Gives weight, body, alcohol and fruit flavours	91, 90	A–D
Cataluña	to soften the more austere Tempranillo grape.	89, 88	
Navarra	NB: Gran Reserva wines are the crème de la	87, 86	
Ribera del Duero	crème, aged at least 3 years in oak	85, 83	
Rioja	and 2 in the bottle before being released for sale. Fuller in style than basic Rioja.	81	
	⌇ 3 years, up to 10 for the best		

Rosé Wines

COUNTRY	COMMENTS		
FRANCE			
Côtes de Provence	Quite heady with fresh, full-flavoured	90, 89	B–C
Lirac	raspberry fruit.	88	
Tavel	⌇ 1 to 3 years. Any longer and they lose their fruit and freshness		
SPAIN			
Navarra	Dry, fruity.	91, 90	A–B
Rioja	⌇ 2 to 4 years	89	

RELIABLE PRODUCERS & SHIPPERS

RED WINES

FRANCE
Languedoc-Roussillon
Corbières – Ch de Cabrane, Ch les Ollieux, Ch St Auriol, Domaine de Fontsainte, Domaine de Reverend
Coteaux du Langeudoc – Ch Rouquette-sur-Mer, Domaine de L'Abbaye Valfernière
Fitou – Caves de Mont-Tauch, Chantovent, Mme Claude Parmentier, Terre Natale
Minervois – Ch le Lastours, Ch les Palais
Northern Rhône
see DOWN THE RHONE VALLEY
Provence
Coteaux d'Aix en Provence – Ch de Beaulieu, Ch de Fonscolombe, Ch la Gaude, Commanderie de la Bargemone, Domaine les Bastides, Marquis de Saporta
Côtes de Provence – Ch Minuty, Commanderie de Peyrassol, Domaine des Hauts de St Jean, Domaine du St Esprit, Domaine Richeaume, La Bernarde, Les Maîtres Vignerons de la Presqu'île de St Tropez, l'Estandon, St Andre de Figuière
Southern Rhône
see DOWN THE RHONE VALLEY

ITALY
Sardinia
Cantina Sociale di Dolianova, Sella e Mosca

SPAIN
Navarra
Bodegas Ochoa, Chivite, Monte Ory, Senorio de Sarria
Ribera del Duero
Cave Co-operative Penafiel, Vega Sicilia
Rioja
Berberana, Bodegas Riojanas, Campo Viejo, El Coto, Faustino, Marques de Caceres, Montecillo, Olarra,

ROSÉ WINES

FRANCE
Lirac
Ch de St Roch, Domaine Maby, Les Queyrades
Provence
Ch de Beaulieu, Ch Simone, Domaine des Hauts de St-Jean, Domaine Gavoty, Domaines Ott, Les Maîtres L'Estandon, Vignerons de la Presqu'île de Saint-Tropez
Tavel
Ch d'Aqueria, Domaine Maby

SPAIN
Navarra
Bodegas Ochoa, Chivite, Monte Ory, Senorio de Sarria

DOWN THE RHONE VALLEY
SYRAH & GRENACHE

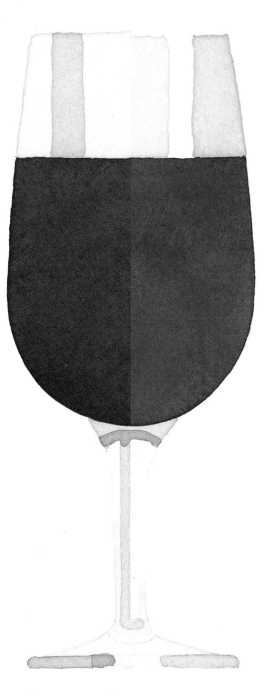

KNOW YOUR GRAPES

The Rhône valley is one of the oldest vineyard areas in France, producing some of its greatest wines – 90% of them red or rosé. Winemaking was recorded here around 600 BC, so there has been plenty of time to establish the right grapes for the area. Many varieties are used but two predominate – Syrah in the north and Grenache in the south.

SYRAH PREDOMINANT
NORTHERN RHONE

In the Northern Rhône, Syrah is the only red grape used. If it is blended, it is with white grapes.

GRENACHE PREDOMINANT
SOUTHERN RHONE

In the Southern Rhône, wines are always blended from red grapes, predominantly Grenache.

FLAVOURS

BLACKCURRANT **BLACKBERRIES**

MIXED SOFT RED FRUITS

SPICY **PEPPER** **HERBS**

Sometimes masked in very ripe vintages when alcohol is high.

With age, wines develop complex flavours of herbs, violets, blackberries, plums, tar, smoke and even burnt rubber! High tannin.

STYLE

LIGHT	MEDIUM	FULL		LIGHT	MEDIUM	FULL
✗	✗	✔		✗	✔	✔

IS IT EVER BLENDED?

Often blended with white grapes. It is not easy to make fine, elegant wines from a single grape variety in a hot climate, but the Northern Rhône is cool enough to make Syrah a viable proposition in its own right.

The warmer climate of the Southern Rhône makes blending essential. A host of grape varieties are used with the predominant Grenache, mainly Syrah, Cinsaut and Mourvèdre.

IS IT OAK-AGED?

Yes

Only for the best wines. Here, the 'macération carbonique' fermentation method is widely used. See WINEMAKING (p.201)

WHEN TO DRINK

Syrah makes big wines so best to leave for at least 3 years, then drink up to 10.

Depends very much on the blend. SEE WHAT'S ON THE SHELVES (p.185).

HOW MUCH WILL IT COST?

B–D   A–D

ARE THE GRAPE NAMES ON THE LABELS?

No   No

KNOW YOUR STYLE

STYLOMETER

S = Syrah – the only red grape
G = Grenache predominant

MEDIUM

G	**Côtes du Rhône**
G	**Côtes du Rhône Villages**
G	**Tricastin**
G	**Côtes du Ventoux**

FULL

G	**Gigondas**
G	**Vacqueyras**
G	**Châteauneuf du Pape**
S	**St Joseph**
S	**Côte Rôtie**
S	**Crozes-Hermitage**
S	**Cornas**
S	**Hermitage**

MAKE THE GRAPE CONNECTION

APPELLATION CONTROLEE

Unlike most other major wine regions of France, the labelling of Rhône wines is comparatively simple. There are three levels of AC in the Rhône, covering both the Northern and the Southern regions. All wines which conform to the regulations for the area are entitled to the basic 'appellation' Côtes du Rhône. Wines which reach higher standards earn the name Côtes du Rhône Villages and those which are judged to be the best are called by their individual village or commune name.

Named VILLAGES or COMMUNES

16 villages with AC COTES DU RHONE VILLAGES

COTES DU RHONE i.e AC for the whole area

GRENACHE PREDOMINANT
SOUTHERN RHONE

Blended with Syrah and other grapes.

COTES DU RHONE VILLAGES
Beaumes de Venise (red)
Cairanne
Chusclan
Laudun
Rasteau
Roaix
Rochegude
Rousset-les-Vignes
Sablet
St Gervais
St Maurice-sur-Eygues
St Pantaléon-les-Vignes
Seguret
Valreas
Vinsobres
Visan

NAMED VILLAGES or COMMUNES
Châteauneuf du Pape
Coteaux du Tricastin
Gigondas
Lirac
Tavel
Vacqueyras

SYRAH
The only red grape in the Northern Rhône.

NAMED VILLAGES or COMMUNES
Cornas
Côte Rôtie
Crozes Hermitage
Hermitage
St Joseph

PLAYING THE GAME

The Rhône produces two quite different tastes from its two major grapes. So, first compare a wine made from the Syrah grape in the north with a Grenache predominant, blended wine from the south.

Game One
Which Grape?

100% Syrah

Grenache
(blended with Syrah and other grapes)

Crozes-Hermitage  **Gigondas** or **Vacqueyras**

A–B 3 years + as Syrah produces full tannic wines

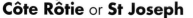

Game Two
Syrah Predominant

If you prefer the taste of Syrah, then stay in the Northern Rhône where it is the only red grape used. A lighter style is produced when white grapes are added in small percentages.

 *Less Full*  *Full*

Côte Rôtie or **St Joseph**  **Crozes-Hermitage** or **Hermitage**

B–C 3 years +

Game Three
Grenache Predominant

As with all wine-growing regions, the wines become more interesting as the vineyard area gets smaller. Here you could compare an 'everyday' wine with one from a named village.

'Everyday' Wine   Village or Commune

Côtes du Rhône **Gigondas**

or   or

Côtes du Ventoux   **Vacqueyras**

A–B   3 years +

Game Four
Grenache Predominant

Now try one of the village wines against a Châteauneuf-du-Pape – of all the Rhône wines, a veritable cocktail of varieties and flavours.

Village or Commune

Gigondas

or   ✔ **Châteauneuf-du-Pape**

Vacqueyras

B–C   not less than 3 years

If you like the underlying flavour and style of Grenache, see p.175 for further comparisons with wines from other parts of the world.

WHAT'S ON THE SHELVES

SYRAH

FULL

COUNTRY	COMMENTS		

NORTHERN RHONE

Cornas — 100% Syrah. Very concentrated, rich, tannic wines with complex flavours and noticeable raspberry.
5 to 10 years — **90, 89 88, 85** — **B–D**

Côte Rôtie — Syrah the only red grape (80% min) with the white Viognier an optional extra. True Syrah, pepper and spice. Delicate with full, concentrated flavour of blackcurrant gums. Very tannic.
3 to 4 years: will keep 5 to10 — **90, 89 88, 85** — **B–D**

Crozes Hermitage — 100% Syrah. A lesser version of the great Hermitage wines.
4 to 10 years — **90, 89 88, 85** — **B–D**

Hermitage — Syrah only red grape with up to 15% Marsanne and Roussanne. One of the great wines of the world. Strong, rich full flavours of blackcurrant and raspberry with pepper and spice overtones.
5 to 10 years+ — **90, 89 88, 85** — **B–D**

St Joseph — Syrah the only red grape with up to 10% white varieties Marsanne and Roussanne. Lightest of Northern Rhône reds. Blackcurrant and raspberry, tannic when young.
3 to 8 years — **90, 89 88, 85** — **B–D**

GRENACHE PREDOMINANT

MEDIUM

COUNTRY	COMMENTS		

SOUTHERN RHONE

Côtes du Rhône	Grenache, Syrah, Cinsaut, Mourvèdre, Carignan and up to 20% other varieties. Fruity. ⊩ 2 to 4 years	90, 89	A
Côtes du Rhône Villages	Grenache (65% maximum), Cinsaut, Syrah and Mourvèdre (25%) and up to 10% all the others. Full, rich and fruity with warm spiciness. Not less than 12.5° alcohol. ⊩ 3 to 6 years	90, 89 88	B
Côtes du Ventoux	Grenache, Cinsaut, Syrah, Mourvèdre. Easy-to-drink, fruity, raspberry-like wines. ⊩ 2 to 4 years	90, 89 88	A
Tricastin	Grenache, Cinsaut, Mourvèdre, Syrah and Carignan (20% max). Full red, rich and fruity. ⊩ 3 to 6 years	90, 89 88	A–B

GRENACHE PREDOMINANT

FULL

COUNTRY	COMMENTS		

SOUTHERN RHONE

COUNTRY	COMMENTS		
Gigondas	Grenache (65% max), Cinsaut, Syrah and Mourvèdre (25% min) and others except Carignan. Big, powerful wines full of flavour and high in alcohol. Developed bouquet of raspberries and blackberries. ⊨▭ 3 to 8 years	90, 89 88, 85	B–D
Vacqueyras	Grenache, Syrah, Cinsaut and Mourvèdre. Similar to Gigondas, big and full. ⊨▭ 3 to 8 years	90, 89 88, 85	B–D
Châteauneuf du Pape	Grenache, Syrah, Cinsaut and Mourvèdre, with the permitted addition of small amounts of other varieties. Château Rayas is the only 100% Grenache and very successful. With 13 permitted grape varieties there is no typical Châteauneuf but all have marvellously complex flavours of herbs, flowers and almonds. Minimum 12.5° alcohol. ⊨▭ 3 to 10 years	90, 89 88, 85	B–D

RELIABLE PRODUCERS & SHIPPERS

SYRAH PREDOMINANT

Cornas
Auguste Clape, Guy de Barjac, Jean Lionnet, Marcel Juge, Robert Michel

Cote Rôtie
Guigal, Jamet, Paul Jaboulet Ainé, Robert Jasmin, Vidal-Fleury

Crozes-Hermitage
Paul Jaboulet Ainé, Tardy et Ange

Hermitage
Chapoutier, Delas, Jean-Louis Chave, Paul Jaboulet Ainé

St Joseph
Chapoutier, Bernard Gripa, Paul Jaboulet Ainé, Emile Florentin,

GRENACHE PREDOMINANT

Châteauneuf-du- Pape
Ch de Beaucastel, Ch de la Nerthe, Ch Fortia, Ch Rayas, Clos des Papes, Clos du Mont Olivet, Domaine Chante-Cigale, Domaine de Mont-Redon, Domaine de Nalys, Domaine du Vieux Télégraphe, Jaboulet Aine, Les Cailloux

Côtes du Rhône
Caves des Vignerons de Rasteau, Ch de Ruth, Ch du Grand Moulas, Cru du Coudoulet, Didier-Charavin, Domaine de la Rengarde, Domaine la Fourmone, Domaine la Soumade, Domaine Rabasse-Charavin, Domaine Ste Estève, Guigal, Jaboulet Ainé, La Serre du Prieur

Côtes du Ventoux
Domaine des Anges, Jaboulet Ainé, La Vieille Ferme

Gigondas
Domaine du Grand Montmirail, Domaine la Fourmone, Domaine Raspail-Ay, Gabriel Meffre, Guigal, Pierre Amadieu

Lirac
Domaine de Castel-Oualou, Domaine de Ch St Roche, Les Queyrades, Maby

FOOD AND WINE

FOOD AND WINE

We often choose a wine just because we enjoy it, and why not? Taste is personal, and there is nothing wrong in eating and drinking what you like, even if it flies in the face of convention. However, some combinations of food and wine work better than others. To understand some of the reasons why, will make it easier to identify a wider range of wines to match or contrast with different foods. It is rash, in our opinion, to be too specific, unless recommending wines to go with difficult foods. Firstly, only *you* know your taste, and secondly, if you do not like the grape, then it is irrelevant whether it suits a particular dish.

When matching food to wine the weight, the level of acidity or tannin (red wines only) and sweetness are more important considerations than colour.

WEIGHT

Weight or body comes from the alcoholic strength, or the amount of fruit and acids. In simple terms, the guts of the wine. A delicate food – fish or meat – will almost certainly be overpowered by a full and rich wine. Conversely a rich, well-seasoned dish will swamp a light and delicate wine.

ACIDITY

Certain foods have a high acidity and make a wine with low acidity taste flat and dull. Matching the acidity will make a better combination. On the other hand, rich dishes or fried foods need wines to 'cut' the richness or fat. Some wines, e.g. Chardonnay, have high acidity ratings although it is not so noticeable as in, say, Sauvignon Blanc, because of their high concentration of fruit. Whether noticeable or not, the acidity is still there and will be a factor when matching food to wine.

TANNIN

The harsh taste of tannin masks the taste of delicate food and with fish, particularly shellfish, it takes on a metallic taste. However, tannin also helps to balance fatty or rich food, so wines high in tannin and acidity complement strongly flavoured or oily dishes.

SWEETNESS AND RICHNESS

These are not identical. A wine to accompany fresh strawberries needs to be sweet but with matching acidity: e.g. a sweet Chenin Blanc or a sweet young Sémillon. Whereas Christmas pudding needs a rich, but not very sweet wine, e.g. a fully mature Sémillon which has lost some of its sweetness with age.

190

SOME GENERAL GUIDELINES

Matching food and wine is not an exact science and sometimes we want to match and sometimes to contrast the flavours. We rarely eat anything with a monotone flavour. The art of matching wine and food is to find the happy compromise. If, very rarely, you come up with the perfect marriage, you will know immediately, just as surely as you know a perfect chord that ends a piece of music or a perfect shot by a great sportsman.

These are just examples of the difficulties – and pleasures – of matching food and wine. Our guidelines may be helpful; but your own experiments and conclusions will be more valuable.

- Aperitifs should stimulate, not satiate, the taste buds, so choose something bracing, crisp and dry. Light Sauvignon Blanc, dry Chenin Blanc, dry English wine, Austrian Veltliner or German Mosel Trocken. If you dislike dry wine, try the French custom of drinking sweet white wines as an aperitif.

- It will normally be the main flavour in sauces that dictates the wine. Delicate fish with a strong sauce will need a stronger wine than plain fish. A Béarnaise sauce needs a light wine with good acidity to match the vinegar in the sauce.

- To show off fine wine, the simplest food is best. Plain grilled fish or roast meat is ideal.

- Wine vinegar is gentler in flavour than malt, which ruins most wines. Instead of mint sauce made with sugar and vinegar, try adding freshly chopped mint to the gravy, or replace vinegar with wine, e.g. in vinaigrette dressing.

- Bread and butter sounds safe enough, but garlic or herb bread, made with melted butter, will overpower any delicate wines.

- Some foods may coat the tongue and therefore are difficult to match with food. Prime examples are chocolate, cream, egg yolk and cheeses such as Camembert and Brie.

Food and Wine Suggestions

Food

Grape Varieties

Fish

Delicate fish
for example cod, halibut, turbot, sole.

Light Chardonnay, Sauvignon Blanc, dry Chenin Blanc, dry German Mosel, Riesling (Trocken).
If you add a slice of lemon to the fish or serve it with a vinegary salad dressing, choose wines with the most acidity. Try fruity red wines with good acidity but low tannin: light Pinot Noir or Beaujolais. High tannin gives a metallic flavour to delicate fish.

Smoked fish
is complemented by wines matured in oak. The oily and positive flavours in some smoke fish go well with spicy, full white wine.

Full, oaked Chardonnay or Sémillon; Gewürztraminer.

Oily or **fried fish**

White or red, with high acidity to cut the oil. Light Chardonnay or Sauvignon Blanc, dry Chenin Blanc, light red Pinot Noir or Beaujolais. Red wines with high tannin may taste metallic.

Shellfish

Why do people say Chablis with shellfish? Because Chablis used to be the English generic word for dry white wine and there was little else to choose from. Today there is a wide choice of dry to medium dry wines – light Chardonnay, dry Chenin Blanc, Muscadet, Vinho Verde. Good acidity is the key.

Crabmeat
is rich and needs a rich wine.

Full Chardonnay or dry Sémillon, medium to full bodied Riesling (dry or medium dry to suit) or Gewürztraminer. This is not a dish to try with red wine.

Food

Pasta

The classic instance where it is the sauce that matters. Plain pasta served with butter or oil will go with most wines. If the pasta if served with a sauce, match the wine to the sauce, for example, tomato sauce is acidic, so match with a higher acidity wine.

Grape Varieties

Red or white, dependent on the sauce. Beaujolais, light red Pinot Noir, red Cabernet Franc from Loire, light Italian.

Meat

Light, white meat, plain veal and roast chicken
will go with most dry wines, red and white.

Red or white but low in alcohol and tannin. Light Pinot Noir, Beaujolais; German Riesling – dry or medium 'sweet to suit – light Gewürztraminer and do not forget rosé.

Lamb
has a certain sweetness which needs a counterbalance of tannin. This applies to all meats with a touch of sweetness.

Cabernet Sauvignon, Syrah/Shiraz, Merlot. Purists claim that a red Bordeaux from Graves or Médoc – where the Cabernet Sauvignon predominates – is the classic combination.

Richly flavoured stews, roast meats, steak and kidney pies
are balanced by good tannin levels.

Grenache, Syrah/Shiraz, Merlot, Cabernet Sauvignon, red Bordeaux.

Meat, fowl or game served with fruit
(duck and orange, pork and apple) needs matching fruitiness in the wine.

Fresh, young and fruity red wines: Beaujolais, Grenache-based wines. Fruity whites, medium dry Riesling.

Fatty meats
need wines with good levels of acidity and plenty of fruit and flavour.

Red or white: full Chardonnays or Sémillons, full dry Riesling, Gewürztraminer. Full Pinot Noir, Beaujolais, red Cabernet Franc from Loire

Game

Full Pinot Noir

Ham
is a salted white meat, if fatty, then serve a red or white wine with good acidity. If lean and plain, try a fruitier red or a sweeter white.

Light Chardonnay, dry Chenin Blanc; Beaujolais, red Cabernet Franc from Loire, medium dry Riesling or Chenin Blanc, Grenache-based wines.

FOOD

VEGETABLES AND SALADS

Individual vegetables: asparagus, artichoke, even cabbage may be 'wine-killers', but blends or mixtures of vegetables are more bland in flavour. Many vegetarian dishes are therefore easy to match with any wine which is not sharp and acid.

DESSERTS

Some desserts just do not go with wine. Chocolate, treacle and citric flavours in general are virtually impossible to match.

Rum, brandy, coffee, citrus and cream flavours go with chocolate, so liqueurs or spirits are usually better than any wine. But a dry, nutty, fortified wine can contrast with the sweetness of a chocolate soufflé and match its bitterness.

For coffee-flavoured creams, and perhaps spicy puddings, much the same applies.

Contrast is less common in matching desserts than in other parts of the meal. However, the French/Italian idea of light, fruity, not too acid, red wine with soft fruit – strawberries, raspberries – is a contrast of flavour. If you do this, try to avoid adding cream.

With fruit pies or flans try to match the amount of acidity in the fruit and the amount of sugar added, to your choice of wine, i.e. choose a high acidity wine if the fruit is also acidic.

GRAPE VARIETIES

Dry Sémillon or dry white Bordeaux (not pure Sauvignon Blanc), dry Riesling (particularly from Pfalz if German). Reds from Grenache-based wines, particularly southern French Vin de Pays.

If you need one, the only resort is fortified wines, or even liqueurs and spirits.

Dry Marsala, dry Oloroso sherry or an old single-quinta port.

Red: young Grenache-based wines (the French say Bordeaux with strawberries). White: for wines with good acidity choose medium sweet or sweet Chenin Blanc or Riesling.

To match sweeter dishes, try sweet Sémillon, or the sweetest Rieslings. Avoid the appley taste of Chenin Blanc with apple desserts.

FOOD

CHEESE

Most hard cheeses match full-flavoured wines – red or white – with low tannin.

Many soft cheeses coat the tongue. They need matching acidity in the wine.

A touch of sweetness can also help. Smoked cheeses respond to a taste of oak or sweetness.

Among the best cheeses to show off fine mature red Bordeaux are mature Dutch Gouda and many of the lesser-known cheeses which are beginning to appear in specialist shops. The rivals are the French equivalents of Cheddar from the Pyrenees, Cantal, etc. Best of all perhaps, the better cheeses of the Gruyère family.

GRAPE VARIETIES

Full Pinot Noir for red wine, full Chardonnays or Sémillons for white.

Red: light Pinot Noir or Beaujolais.
White: Chenin Blanc, medium dry/sweet.

Oak: full Chardonnays.
Sweetness: Sémillon, sweet Riesling.

Red Bordeaux, Cabernet Sauvignon, Merlot.

Food

Spicy Food

Curry is usually best with beer or water but a full wine with plenty of flavour is a good match.

Chinese: Sugar is the problem and it is obvious in sweet and sour sauces, less obvious in many other dishes. The many spices used can also kill refined wine flavours. Sometimes one must admit that beer is best. Even if you avoid sweet and sour, the matching of Chinese food is unlike that of European. Meat and fish are often present in the one dish, and flavours are modified by special methods. Fish rarely tastes fishy, because 'de-fishing' ingredients, including ginger, rice wine and the skins of citrus fruits are freely used. These are some of the problems. With deep-fried food acidity helps to cut the oiliness. With stir-fried and steamed dishes, a full, deep flavoured white. Stews and casseroles usually need a full flavoured red and, even if oily or greasy, this seems to work.

Japanese and Thai: Very few people (except Japanese) try to produce Japanese food at home. Thai spice packs are just beginning to appear. With Thai food, strong flavoured, crisp white wine is required.

Grape Varieties

Gewürztraminer – four or five year old – Merlot. Avoid wine with mango chutney; this really is a killer.

Choosing The Wine

Each grape variety has its own character and some produce more tannin or acidity than others. Therefore it may help you to follow the guidelines by using the chart below which shows the average levels of acidity, tannin (red wines only) and alcohol in the major grape varieties.

ACIDITY, TANNIN AND ALCOHOL LEVELS

RED GRAPES	Acidity Scale 1–10	Tannin Scale 1–10	Alcohol % Vol
CABERNET SAUVIGNON			
Australia	4	7–9	11–13 +
Bordeaux	4–5	6–8	12–13
Bulgaria	4	5	12–13
Chile	4	5	12
South Africa	4	6	12–13
Tuscany	5	6	12–13
GAMAY			
Beaujolais	5	3	12–13
Loire	6	4	12–13
GRENACHE			
Rhône	4	7	12–14
Rioja	4	6	12–13
MERLOT			
Bordeaux	4	6	12–13
California	4	7	13
Croatia	3	7	11–13
Hungary	3	5	12
Italy	4	6	12
Slovenia	3	7	11–13
PINOT NOIR			
Alsace	6	2	11–12
California	4	4	12–13 +
Côte d'Or	5	3	12–13 +
Hungary	4	2	12
Loire	6	3	11–12
Oregon	5	4	12–13 +
SYRAH			
Australia	3	10	11–14
Rhône	3	8–9	12–14

ACIDITY, TANNIN AND ALCOHOL LEVELS

WHITE GRAPES (No noticeable tannin)	ACIDITY Scale 1–10	ALCOHOL % Vol
CHARDONNAY		
Alto-Adige	6	12
Australia (Hunter Valley & Victoria)	8–10	11–13
California	8–10	13
Chablis	9	13
Chile	6	12
Côte d'Or	8–9	13
New Zealand	10	13 +
Spain	5	12
CHENIN BLANC		
California	7	12
Loire	8–10	12
New Zealand	7	12
South Africa	7	12
GEWURZTRAMINER		
Alsace	6–8	12–13
California	6	11
Germany	6–8	11
New Zealand	6	11
RIESLING		
Alsace	8	11
Alto-Adige	6	11
Australia (Rhien Riesling)	6	12
California (Johannisberg Riesling)	6	12
Germany: Rhein	*8–10	8–11
Mosel	*9–10	8–11

* **NB:** Eiswein can be much more acidic – up to 14–15 on this scale

	ACIDITY Scale 1–10	ALCOHOL % Vol
SAUVIGNON BLANC		
Bordeaux	6	12
California	8–9	12–13
Chile	6	12
New Zealand (North & South Island)	8–9	12–13
Sancerre	9	12
SEMILLON		
Australia – dry	5	12
– sweet	7	11–14
Bordeaux – dry	5	12
– sweet	7	13

USEFUL INFORMATION
STYLE
QUALITY WINE
READING WINE LABELS
SERVING WINE

STYLE

What is in a Grape?

The five basic constituents common to all wines are:

1 Fruit

The essence of the crushed grape which carries its character and distinctive aroma and flavour. Apart from the climate, the concentration of fruit helps to determine whether the wine is light, medium or full-bodied.

2 Acidity

Acidity sounds very unattractive but the natural acids found in the grape are essential to wine. Keeping it fresh, acting as a preservative and prolonging the taste. You can feel them at the back and underneath of the tongue.

Some grapes, such as Sauvignon Blanc, have more natural acidity than others, e.g. Sémillon. Other grapes like Chardonnay often have as much natural acidity as Sauvignon Blanc but the richer fruit makes the acidity less noticeable. Acidity only becomes unpleasant when the wine is unbalanced.

3 Alcohol

The yeasts in the grape convert the grape sugars into alcohol by fermentation. Fermentation stops naturally when all the sugar has been converted, or the level of alcohol has reached 14° or 15°, at which point the yeast is killed. Any sugar remaining produces a naturally sweet wine. Sweet wines are also made artificially by adding alcohol to the 'must' – the crushed grapes – thus stopping the fermentation and leaving residual sugar.

4 Tannin

Tannin is a useful preservative, often found in tea and detected by an astringest, bitter dryness on the tongue and at the back of the teeth. It comes largely from the grape skins, so is barely noticeable, if at all, in white wines, which are usually fermented without the skins. Tannin will always be present in young red wines intended for ageing and is more noticeable in some varieties, e.g. Syrah/Shiraz and Cabernet Sauvignon. Tannin diminishes as the wine ages and should almost disappear once the wine is fully matured. It is sometimes described as soft, i.e. not aggressive, in wines from warmer regions.

5 Water

Water is about 85° to 90° of the natural volume of a bottle of wine, the rest is alcohol. It is illegal to add water to wine.

'Weight' or 'Body'

The weight or body of a wine comes from a combination of:

    Alcohol
    Fruit
    Acids

In simple terms, the guts of a wine.

A Chablis (100% French Chardonnay) of say 12.5° may have exactly the same level of alcohol as an Australian Chardonnay, but the greater concentration of fruit and acidity in the Australian wine gives it more weight.

Apart from alcohol, weight or body is to a certain degree dependent on the pruning of the vine and the amount of water it receives, naturally or artificially. The more irrigation, the more lush the grapes and the lower the concentration of fruit because the water content is higher. The more the bunches are pruned and small grapes removed, the more concentrated the flavours and thus, the greater the weight.

Pressing also has an effect. The more the grapes are pressed, the higher the yield and the lower the weight. Like the finest olive oil, the best wines are pressed only once, which is why they have more weight. For example Château Lafite may have exactly the same amount of alcohol as a plain Bordeaux Rouge, but it will have infinitely more body and command a far higher price.

WINEMAKING

Winemakers, particularly those in many European wine regions, are constantly faced with less than perfect conditions at harvest time. Their skill has to balance some of nature's shortcomings and excesses, which often produces very acceptable wines from unpromising material.

Winemaking skills have improved out of all recognition during the last 20 years. This has been spurred on by the example and success of fairly new winemakers in North America, South Africa and Australasia. In Europe, as the new generation take over the vineyards and wineries, these modern techniques are being used to improve the quality and character of the wine we drink.

Today, as wine drinking becomes more widespread, the emphasis is less and less on mass-produced wine and increasingly on Quality wine. This need not be expensive, as Bulgaria and Australia have proved. The good winemakers who are competing in the international arena will always sacrifice volume for quality.

The grape variety and the climate play a vital part in shaping flavour and style but, without the winemakers, there would be a boring similarity to most wines. It is the winemaker who decides how much of each to use when making a blend from two or more grape varieties. Whether to mature in oak or tank, or to make wines which mature quickly or slowly. With some varieties – notably Riesling, Sémillon and Chenin Blanc – the winemaker even decides whether the wine will be dry, medium or sweet. All these decisions and many others affect the final taste.

The winemaker's skill in handling the raw material is vital. In horseracing terms, you may own a potential Derby winner but whether it wins the race or not will almost certainly depend on the skill of the trainer.

The Key to a Good Wine...
...is Balance

A good wine is said to be 'well-balanced' when all the constituents are in the right proportions. It will have good fruit flavours and leave a positive taste in the mouth. The older the wine, the more mellow the fruit and the softer, more lingering the 'after-taste' or 'finish'. Wine trade words which are hard to replace.

Nature has a habit, in both cool and warm climates, of providing less than perfect growing conditions, so winemakers are regularly correcting its shortcomings and excesses.

Using sophisticated techniques, winemakers also force wines to mature quickly or slowly, control the alcohol levels and produce fresh wines by maturing them in steel or glass-lined tanks. Fuller and more complex wines are still produced by ageing them in oak barrels or vats.

Wines for early drinking must be balanced from the outset. Fine wines need time to mature in the bottle – more for reds than whites – before balance is achieved.

Climate

The Stylometer shows that cool regions also exist in the warmest countries. These cool climate wines suffer from all the risks which face western European wine growers: too much or too little rain, not enough or too much sun, frost, hail, etc. Modern technology enables the winemaker to overcome some of nature's stumbling blocks.

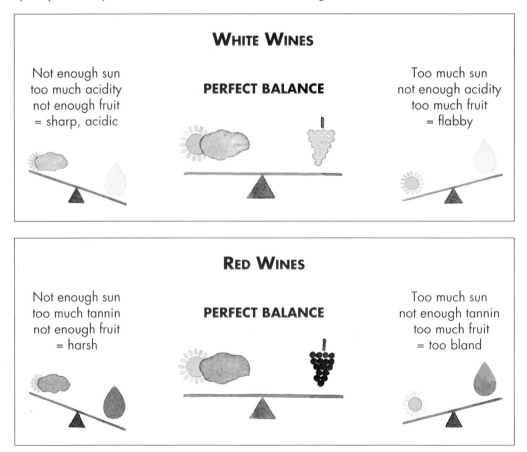

WHITE WINES

Not enough sun
too much acidity
not enough fruit
= sharp, acidic

PERFECT BALANCE

Too much sun
not enough acidity
too much fruit
= flabby

RED WINES

Not enough sun
too much tannin
not enough fruit
= harsh

PERFECT BALANCE

Too much sun
not enough tannin
too much fruit
= too bland

In unusually hot weather, the winemaker will harvest earlier when the balance of fruit and acidity is correct. Otherwise the grapes will be very ripe, with plenty of sugar but lacking acidity. The wines will be powerful and alcoholic but without enough acidity they will taste uninteresting and flabby. The winemaker may also acidify the wine. Perfectly legal if permitted acids are used in harmless and prescribed amounts.

If the weather has been cold, alcohol levels will be too low. A common solution is chaptalisation. If the wine is unbalanced and too high in acidity – common in poor years – unfermented grape juice, Süssreserve, is sometimes added to provide a counterbalance of sweetness.

SOIL

Vines do not like wet feet! So it is important that the soil it grows in drains well. This forces the roots down – often many metres – in search of moisture and makes the vine less susceptable to the weather conditions on the surface.

The longer it takes for a grape to ripen (the growing season), the more refined and elegant the style of the wine.

In cool climates, the usual problem is that, particularly in poor years, the grapes are not fully ripe. A soil which retains heat is clearly a bonus because it will help to speed the ripening process. A prime example is the gravelly soil of the Graves and Médoc in Bordeaux, where the late ripening Cabernet Sauvignon is predominantly planted.

In warm or hot climates, a cool soil is important because it helps to slow down the ripening process and prolongs the growing season.

Just how much influence a particular soil has on the ultimate flavour and style of a wine is hotly debated.

MAKING A WINE DRY OR SWEET

A dry wine is produced when all the natural sugar in the grape has been fermented out and turned into alcohol. In hot climates, grapes are often picked early to keep the sugar content in the grapes as low as possible.

Fermentation will cease when a wine reaches 15° of alcohol, so a naturally sweet wine is made when there is residual sugar left in the 'must' (crushed grapes) after fermentation has finished. Sweet wine is also produced by:
- raising the alcohol and artificially stopping the fermentation, thus leaving the required amount of residual sugar.
- adding Süssreserve (unfermented grape juice) to the fermented wine. There are complicated rules controlling the use of Süssreserve in Germany, where it may be added up to Auslese level. Basically, it must be of the same quality as the wine to which it is added and where possible, from the same region. How much is used is another matter. Wherever this technique is used, too much Süssreserve swamps the acidity and the wines become sweet and characterless.

FERMENTATION

Wines are fermented and matured either in oak barrels or vats or in steel/glass-lined tanks. Both methods produce excellent wines. Some winemakers prefer to use oak barrels or vats, even though they are difficult and expensive to clean thoroughly and control fermentation. Each method produces its own style and in the end it is purely a matter of personal choice which you prefer.

In the past, fermentation has often been a hit-and-miss affair. Until the 1950s, fires were lit under the fermentation vats if the temperature fell too low and blocks of ice packed round them if it became too high. Today the operation is far more up-to-date, using high-tech equipment to control temperatures, which is so important to ensure the freshness of white wines and to develop the flavour and character of the reds.

Macération Carbonique

A comparatively recent technique. Grapes are put uncrushed into a closed steel/glass-lined vat and allowed to ferment with their skins. This way they retain all the fruit flavours and freshness which make such wines as Beaujolais and Côtes du Rhone such delightful drinks. It is a technique particularly suited to producing wines for early drinking. The labels do not tell you when this method is used.

Maturing Wine Before Bottling

After fermentation has finished, most young wines need time to mature before bottling. The amount of time depends on its quality and style. Inexpensive, easy-to-drink wines – particularly whites – will be ready for immediate consumption as soon as bottled. Anything from 6 to 18 months after the vintage. Fuller, higher quality wines, will require more time in the bottle, after their initial maturation period, before they are ready to drink.

Maturing in Steel or Glass-lined Tanks

These are used worldwide to produce fresh, fruity styles and are particularly suitable for inexpensive, early drinking wines. They will never make the rich, complex wines which result from a degree of oak-ageing.

Maturing in Wood

Wine, particularly red wine, has traditionally been aged in oak barrels or vats. New oak adds complexity and depth of flavour, increasing the cost and adding to the tannin content, so its use must be carefully gauged.

Most white grapes produce wines which are best when young and fresh, so only a few – notably Chardonnay and Sémillon – benefit from oak ageing and then only the best .

Too much oak-flavour, particularly from new woods, masks the fruit and leaves. Most Europeans use oak with subtlety whereas some 'new world' winemakers have tended towards a more overt flavour. Now that they have a growing market in Europe, many of the best winemakers are using less oak to produce a more elegant and refined style.

In some eastern European countries, oak-ageing is a fundamental part of winemaking for all wines. However, the containers are large and usually old and are used more for storage than to impart any oak flavour.

Winemakers around the world differ in opinion on which method to use, so styles of wine, even from the same grape, may vary considerably. Frustratingly – with the exception of Australasia, South Africa and the Americas – the label rarely tells you whether tanks or oak barrels have been used.

'Noble Rot' or Botrytis Cinerea

The secret of the marvellous balance between sweetness and dryness in great dessert wines such as Sauternes and Barsac is the existence of a benign fungus which affects the grapes called 'botrytis cinerea' or 'pourriture noble' in France. The ideal conditions for producing the fungus are misty autumn mornings followed by warm sunny afternoons. The grapes shrivel from the rot which in turn concentrates the juice and is then pressed out gently to produce a luscious golden wine with honeyed flavours. The natural acidity in the wine prevents it from becoming too cloying, producing a sweetness that is more of fresh fruit than fruit syrup.

These conditions are found in Bordeaux, Bergerac, the Loire and occasionally Alsace regions of France. In Europe, 'noble rot' also appears in Germany. In warmer climates, the grapes are ripe enough to produce dessert wines without 'noble rot' but it is still found in Australia and parts of South Africa and California.

INCREASING THE STRENGTH OR CHAPTALISATION

In cool climates, the grapes will not always have enough sugar to produce the required amount of alcohol so, to produce a drinkable wine, the 'must' (crushed grapes) is enriched with sugar to raise the strength through fermentation. This is common – and legal – practice in many wine growing areas but there are usually strict rules. For example in Burgundy, the final strength after the addition of sugar must never exceed the maximum level permitted for each region, village or top vineyard. In Germany, Chaptalisation is permitted for the lower level of QbA wines only. See RIESLING – GERMANY (p.47).

VINTAGE

The vintage date on a label refers to the year in which the grapes were harvested and turned into wine. North of the Equator the growing season is between March and October and the harvest follows on immediately. South of the Equator the harvest takes place from January to March, so the growing season is mainly in the previous year. Thus a bottle from Australia labelled 1990 is almost the same age as a wine from Europe or North America dated 1989.

The style and quality of the wine in large depends on the weather during the growing season. In the warmer parts of the world the weather is usually constant, so there is little difference between one year and the next and vintages are really just an indication of age. In cooler climates the weather is often less reliable, so vintages are an indication of style and quality, as well as age.

The good vintages shown in each guide are general recommendations only, because a good winemaker can occasionally produce very good wine in a poor year and equally, poor winemakers can make a bad wine in a good year.

When comparing wines, it is usually best to choose them from the same vintages, particularly if they come from parts of the world where the climate is variable.

QUALITY WINE

Wine is made the world over. Some of it is excellent, some good and the rest is either ordinary or poor. As yet, there is no international code or standard for describing wine, and regulations vary from country to country.

WHAT IS QUALITY WINE?

Any wine that is made from a specified grape or grapes and comes from a clearly defined region is Quality wine. So, how do you identify Quality wine from the label?

HOW TO FIND QUALITY WINES ON THE SHELVES

In most countries, you will recognise Quality wine easily because the grape variety and the region are clearly shown on the label.

Within the EC, it is not always so easy, because many Quality wines do not show the grape name – only the region – on the label. You can identify them by quality classifications which must be shown on the label (see list on opposite page). For each country the standard quality is listed first, followed by the higher quality.

COUNTRY WINES

A new group of wines is spreading through the EC and where relevant, we include them. They still come from a clearly defined region but they may be made from grapes new to the region. The controls are less strict, so these are mainly inexpensive wines for early drinking. They will have one of the following descriptions

on the label, always followed by the name of the region:

COUNTRY	LABELLED AS
FRANCE	Vin de Pays
GERMANY	Landwein
ITALY	Vino Tipico
PORTUGAL	Vinho Regionão
SPAIN	Vino de la Tierra

WHICH WINES ARE NOT QUALITY WINE?

These are wines which are made from unspecified grapes, grown anywhere and with minimal regulations regarding volume, strength and methods of vinification and which have no regional or grape varietal character. They are the cheapest of the world's wines, blended and manufactured to a chosen taste so we do not include them.

TABLE WINE

In the EC, Table wine must have the following description on the label:

COUNTRY	DESCRIPTION
FRANCE	Vin de Table
GERMANY	Deutsche Tafelwein
ITALY	Vino da Tavola
PORTUGAL	Vinho de Mesa
SPAIN	Vino de Mesa

'BRANDS'

For 'brands' read bland! 'Brands' are mass-produced, usually heavily advertised wines designed for the mass market and made to the instructions of marketing men to produce inoffensive wines. They should never vary in style. At best – usually the few with a Quality rating – they are acceptable but comparatively expensive, e.g. Hirondelle, Piat d'Or, Black Tower.

HOW TO FIND QUALITY WINES ON THE SHELVES

LABELLED AS	WINE LISTS MAY INDICATE AS

AUSTRIA
Qualitätswein bestimmter Anbaugebiete — **QbA**
Qualitätswein mit Prädikat — **QmP**

BULGARIA
Wine of declared origin — **DGO**
Controliran (better wine within the DGO) — **Controliran**

FRANCE
Vin délimité de Qualité Supérieure — **VDQS**
Appellation d'Origine Contrôlée — **AOC** or **AC**

GERMANY
Qualitätswein bestimmter Anbaugebiete — **QbA**
Qualitätswein mit Prädikat — **QmP**

GREECE
Appellation d'Origine Contrôlée — **AOC** or **AC**

ITALY
Denominazione di Origine Controllata — **DOC**
Demominazione di Origine Controllata e Garantita — **DOCG**
Some wines do not qualify for a DOC/DOCG
rating because the grapes are not specified for
the region. Although they are labelled as Table wines
(Vino da Tavola), we count them as Quality wine.
They can be identified by the noticeably high price.

PORTUGAL
Região Demarcado — **RD**

SOUTH AFRICA
Wine of origin
(The best wines have all three bands) —
Blue band on neck = certified region
Red band on neck = certified vintage
Green band on neck = certified grape variety

SPAIN
Denominación de Origen — **DO**

READING WINE LABELS

The grape or grapes, together with the region of origin, primarily dictate the taste of a wine, but many labels – notably French – only give the region. Those from Germany are often long-winded and usually daunting to read due to their Gothic script. We show here how to interpret French and German regional labels, and also an example of how much easier it is to identify taste when the label shows both grapes and region.

FRENCH QUALITY WINE
LABELLING BY REGION

Guarantee that the wine is 100% from grapes grown in Sancerre

Name and address of estate and producer

Where wine was bottled – in this instance at the property (domaine)

Country of origin

Parish or commune where grapes were grown

Minimum amount of wine in bottle

It is not on the label, but the grape is 100% Sauvignon Blanc

GERMAN QUALITY WINE
LABELLING BY REGION AND GRAPE VARIETY

Name and address of producer

Region in which grapes were grown

Berg Roseneck is the vineyard name

Year in which grapes were grown and wine was made

Name of village = Rudesheim (the 'er' on the end means 'of Rudesheim')

Name of grape

Type of wine: Spätlese means late picked, thus a wine that is medium sweet

Top category of German quality wine – 'mit Prädikat' meaning 'with distinction'

Estate bottled

Quality control number – every bottle of German quality wine has an AP number (Amtliche Prufungsnummer)

AUSTRALIAN QUALITY WINE
LABELLING BY REGION AND GRAPE VARIETY

Producer's name

Grapes used – predominant variety named first

Name of vineyard and State in which grapes were grown

Name and address of producer

Minimum amount of wine in bottle

Year when wine was made

Strength of wine

Country of origin

209

Serving Wine

Temperature

White wines should be chilled – not frozen. One hour in the fridge is enough. When chilling sparkling wine in the fridge, always keep the bottle lying down. There is far more chance of the bottle exploding if it has been standing up.

Red wines should be tasted at room temperature. Just leave the bottles in a warm room for a day or two before using. If you have left it late, you could put a cold bottle in warm water for half an hour, at least this is better than putting it by the oven to cook!

Tasting Glasses

Ideally they should be tulip-shaped to capture the wine's aroma as you swirl it around – but any will do!

Serving Red and White Wines

White wines may be served immediately after opening. Uncork red wines an hour or so before drinking. Better still, pour them gently into a decanter or jug. Wines get a bit jaded after being cooped up in the bottle and even the most ordinary benefit from a breath of fresh air.

Decanting

After four or five years in the bottle, some wines produce a sediment. This is not only unsightly but can also harm the taste, so it is important to remove it by decanting. The process is really very simple but to be successful, it should never be hurried.

Stand the bottle upright for a few days before drinking. This allows the sediment to fall to the bottom of the bottle. If from previous experience, you know that the sediment in a particular wine is quite light, it may need only a day, but it is better to be safe than sorry, for decanting will never remove sediment that is right through the wine. The only way to over-come this problem is to decant through filter paper.

About an hour or so before drinking, pull the cork very carefully so as not to disturb the sediment. This allows the wine to 'breathe' and rid itself of any smells that come from being cooped up in the bottle.

Some bottles are dirty around the cork when the

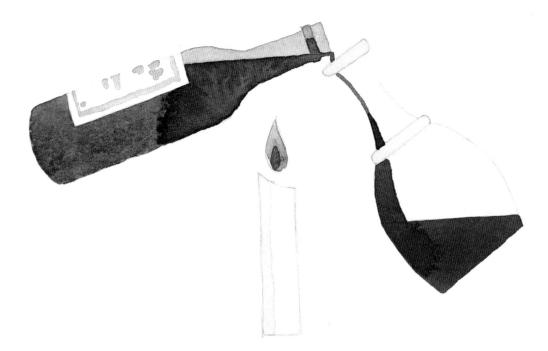

lead cap is removed. It is important to wipe the top with a clean cloth or the wine becomes tainted as you pour.

Place a lit candle between the hand you pour with and the decanter. Then, slowly and carefully, pour the wine into the decanter with the candle shining through the neck of the bottle. Look into the bottle through the candlelight and you will see the sediment when it reaches the neck. This is the moment to stop pouring. If you have done your stuff correctly, there should be no more than a quarter of a glass left in the bottle!

If you do not stand the bottle up in time, decant with the bottle lying on its side. This is a more delicate operation however and requires a cradle or device to raise the neck of the bottle and prevent the wine spilling out as the cork is drawn. Otherwise, the process is the same.

RECORKING

Air is the great enemy of wine. If you do not finish the bottle, it will keep for 24 hours if you recork firmly. One of the clever sealing devices on the market will keep it even longer. Store the resealed-recorked bottle in a cool place.

WINE MERCHANTS

The leading supermarket chains offer a good range of wines from all over the world and have forced many high-street multiples to improve their range, so you should find most of the wine we cover without too much difficulty.

We indicate specialists for the rarer or less well known wines, because they are limited in quantity and therefore unsuitable for mass distribution. However, our selection covers most of those who have a good, representative choice of the wines covered in the guides.

GENERAL
fine wine merchants with an extensive list from most parts of the world

Adnams
  Southwold, Suffolk: 0502 724222
Avery's of Bristol
  Bristol: 0272 214141
Berry Bros & Rudd
  London SW1: 071 839 9033
Bibendum
  London NW1: 071 586 9761
Corney & Barrow
  London EC1 : 071 251 4051
Eldridge Pope
  Dorchester, Dorset : 0305 251251
Findlater Mackie Todd
  London SW19: 081 543 0966
John Harvey & Sons
  Bristol: 0272 253253
Harrods
  London SW1: 071 730 1234
Haynes Hanson & Clark
  London SW6: 071 736 7878
S H Jones
  Banbury, Oxon: 0295 251178
Justerini & Brooks
  London SW1: 071 493 8721
  Edinburgh: 031 226 4202

Lay & Wheeler
  Colchester, Essex: 0206 764446
Thos Peatling
  Bury St Edmunds, Suffolk:
  0284 755948
Arthur Rackham
  Byfleet, Surrey: 09323 51585
Robeson
  London W14: 071 371 2121
Russell & McIver
  London EC3: 071 283 3575
Selfridges
  London W1: 071 629 1234
Tanners Wines
  Shrewsbury, Salop: 0743 232007
J Townend & Sons
  Hull, Humberside: 0482 26891
Willoughbys
  Manchester: 061 834 6850

COUNTRY OR REGIONAL SPECIALISTS

AUSTRALIA

David Alexander
  Maidenhead, Berks: 0628 30295
D Byrne & Co
  Clitheroe, Lancs: 0200 23152
The Celtic Vintner
  Swansea, Glam. : 0792 206661
City Wines
  Norwich, Norfolk: 0603 617967
Claridge Fine Wines
  Hawkenbury, Kent: 0580 893303
Alex Findlater
  Halesworth, Suffolk: 0986 83274
Oddbins
  national stockist
Raeburn Fine Wines
  Edinburgh: 031 332 5166
La Reserva Wines
  Huddersfield, Yorks: 0484 846732

AUSTRIA

Premier Wines
  Stevenston, Ayrshire: 0294 602409
A L Vose
  Grange-over-Sands, Cumbria:
  05395 33328

BULGARIA

The Celtic Vintner
  Swansea: 0792 206661
Wines of Westhorpe
  Marchington, Staffs: 0283 820285

CHILE

Hedley Wright
  Bishops Stortford, Herts: 0279 506512

FRANCE

Alsace
Anthony Byrne Fine Wines
  Ramsey, Cambs: 0487 814555
D Byrne & Co
  Clitheroe, Lancs: 0200 23152
Peter Green
  Edinburgh: 031 229 5925
J E Hogg
  Edinburgh: 031 556 4025
O W Loeb
  London SE1: 071 928 7750
The Upper Crust
  East Horsley, Surrey: 04865 3280
La Vigneronne
  London SW7: 071 589 6113

Beaujolais
Anthony Byrne Fine Wines
  Ramsey, Cambs: 0487 814555
Berkmann Wine Cellars
  London N7: 081 609 4711
Roger Harris
  Weston Longville, Norfolk:
  0603 880171

Ian G Howe
  Newark, Notts: 0636 704366
Arthur Rackham
  Byfleet, Surrey: 09323 51585
The Upper Crust
  East Horsley, Surrey: 04865 3280

Bordeaux
John Armit Wines
  London W11: 071 727 6846
Ballantynes
  Cowbridge, Glamorgan: 04463 3044
D Byrne & Co
  Clitheroe, Lancs: 0200 23152
Cadwgan Fine Wine Merchants
  Altrincham, Cheshire: 061 928 0357
Cairns & Hickey
  Leeds, Yorks: 05321 459501
Davisons Wine Merchants
  Croydon, Surrey: 081 681 3222
Farr Vintners
  London SW1: 071 630 5348
Haynes Hanson & Clark
  London SW6: 071 736 7878
Hungerford Wine Co
  Hungerford, Berks: 0488 83238
La Reserve
  London SW1: 071 589 2020
Laytons
  London NW1: 071 388 5081
O W Loeb
  London SE1: 071 928 7750
Master Cellar Wine Warehouse
  Croydon, Surrey: 081 686 9989
Michael Menzel
  Sheffield, Yorks: 0742 683557
Nickolls & Perks
  Stourbridge, West Midlands:
  0384 394518
Supergrape
  London SW18: 081 874 5963
The Upper Crust
  East Horsley, Surrey: 04865 3280
Michael Menzel
  Sheffield, Yorks: 0742 683557
T & W Wines
  Thetford, Norfolk: 0842 765646
La Vigneronne
  London SW7: 071 589 6113

Whittals Wines
Walsall, West Midlands: 0922 36161

Burgundy

Ballantynes of Cowbridge
Cowbridge, Glamorgan: 04463 3044
Berkmann Wine Cellars
London N7: 081 609 4711
Anthony Byrne Fine Wines
Ramsey, Cambs: 0487 814555
D Byrne & Co
Clitheroe, Lancs: 0200 23152
Christchurch Fine Wine Co
Christchurch, Dorset: 0202 473255
Farr Vintners
London SW1: 071 630 5348
Haynes Hanson & Clark
London SW6: 071 736 7878
Hungerford Wine Co
Hungerford, Berks: 0488 83238
Ingletons Wines
Maldon, Essex: 0621 852431
Laytons
London NW1: 071 388 5081
O W Loeb
London SE1: 071 928 7750
Michael Menzel
Sheffield, Yorks: 0742 683557
Morris & Verdin
London SW1: 071 630 8888
Nickolls & Perks
Stourbridge, West Midlands:
0384 394518
Howard Ripley
London N21: 081 360 8904
The Upper Crust
East Horsley, Surrey: 04865 3280
T & W Wines
Thetford, Norfolk: 0842 765646
La Vigneronne
London SW7: 071 589 6113
Whittals Wines
Walsall, West Midlands: 0922 36161

Loire

Anthony Byrne Fine Wines
Ramsey, Cambs: 0487 814555
Chesterford Vintners
Great Chesterford, Essex: 0799 30088

Christchurch Fine Wine Co
Christchurch, Dorset: 0202 473255
Peter Green
Edinburgh: 031 229 5925
Ian G Howe
Newark, Notts: 0636 704366
The Upper Crust
East Horsley, Surrey: 04865 3280
Yapp Brothers
Mere Wilts: 0747 860423

Rhône

Anthony Byrne Fine Wines
Ramsey, Cambs: 0487 814555
Cadwgan Fine Wine Merchants
Altrincham, Cheshire: 061 928 0357
Christchurch Fine Wine Co
Christchurch, Dorset: 0202 473255
Domaine Direct
London WC1: 071 837 3521
Farr Vintners
London SW1: 071 630 5348
Michael Menzel
Sheffield, Yorks: 0742 683557
Sapsford Wines
Ware, Herts: 0920 467040
T & W Wines
Thetford, Norfolk: 0842 765646
La Vigneronne
London SW7: 071 589 6113
Whittals Wines
Walsall, West Midlands: 0922 36161
Yapp Brothers
Mere, Wilts: 0747 860423

South West
(Bergerac, Côtes de Buzet, Cahors, Côtes du Frontonnais, Madiran and Vins de Pays)

Desborough & Brown Fine Wines
St Albans, Herts: 0727 44449

GERMANY

D Byrne & Co
Clitheroe, Lancs: 0200 23152
Dennhöfer Wines
Newcastle on Tyne: 091 232 7342

Alex Findlater
    Halesworth, Suffolk: 0986 83274
Douglas Henn-Macrae
    Maidstone, Kent: 0622 710952
J E Hogg
    Edinburgh: 031 556 4025
O W Loeb
    London SE1: 071 928 7750

HUNGARY

Wines of Westhorpe
    Marchington, Staffs: 0283 820285

ITALY

Ad Hoc Wine Warehouse
    London SW9: 081 326 1799
D Byrne & Co
    Clitheroe, Lancs: 0200 23152
Alex Findlater
    Halesworth, Suffolk: 0986 83274
Peter Green
    Edinburgh: 031 229 5925
J E Hogg
    Edinburgh: 031 556 4025
Millevini
    Stockport, Lancs: 0663 64366
Valvona & Crolla
    Edinburgh: 031 556 6066
Windrush Wines
    Cirencester, Glos: 0285 650466
Wine Growers Association
    London NW10: 081 451 0981

NEW ZEALAND

City Wines
    Norwich, Norfolk: 0603 617967
Claridge Fine Wines
    Hawkenbury, Kent: 0580 893303
J C Karn
    Cheltenham, Glos: 0242 513265
La Reserva Wines
    Huddersfield, Yorks: 0484 846732

SPAIN

A & A Wines
    Cranleigh, Surrey: 0483 274666
Ad Hoc Wine Warehouse
    London SW9: 071 326 1799
Arriba Kettle
    Evesham Hereford & Worcs:
    0386 833024
Bottle & Basket
    London N6: 081 341 7018
Laymont & Shaw
    Truro, Cornwall: 0872 70545
Martinez Fine Wine
    Ikley, Yorks: 0943 603241
Mi Casa Wines
    Buxton, Derbyshire: 0298 3952
Moreno Wines
    London W9: 071 286 0678
La Reserva Wines
    Huddersfield, Yorks: 0484 846732
Sherborne Vintners
    Sherborne, Dorset: 0935 873033
The Wine House
    Wallington, Surrey: 081 669 6661

USA

California
Les Amis du Vin
    London W1: 071 636 4020
Haughton Fine Wines
    Nantwich, Cheshire: 0270 74537
Oddbins
    National stockists
T & W Wines
    Thetford, Norfolk: 0842 765646
Windrush Wines
    Cirencester, Glos: 0285 650466

Oregon & Washington State

Haughton Fine Wines
    Nantwich, Cheshire: 0270 7453
Douglas Henn-Macrae
    Maidstone, Kent: 0622 710952
Windrush Wines
    Cirencester, Glos: 0285 650466

RECOMMENDED BOOKS

The books listed below are published in the UK, unless otherwise indicated.

GENERAL

White Wine Guide/Red Wine Guide
(2 volumes)
Jim Ainsworth
Mitchell Beazley, 1990

New Encyclopaedia of Wine
Alexis Bespaloff
Random Century, 1990

Pocket Guide to Wine Tasting
Michael Broadbent
Mitchell Beazley, 1991

Wine Factfinder and Taste Guide
Oz Clarke
Mitchell Beazley, 1989

Wine Guide 1992
Oz Clarke
Webster, 1991

Wines of the World
Oz Clarke
Sainsbury, 1988

How to Enjoy Your Wine
Hugh Johnson
Mitchell Beazley, 1991

Pocket Wine Book
Hugh Johnson
Mitchell Beazley, 1991

The Story of Wine
Hugh Johnson
Mitchell Beazley, 1990 hardback;
1991 paperback

Wine Companion
Hugh Johnson
Mitchell Beazley, 1991

World Atlas of Wine
Hugh Johnson
Mitchell Beazley 1990

Good Wine Guide
Robert Joseph
published annually by
The Daily Telegraph

The Taste of Wine
Emile Peynaud
Macdonald Orbis, 1992

Vines, Grapes, Wines
Jancis Robinson
Mitchell Beazley, 1986

Vintage Time Charts
Jancis Robinson
Mitchell Beazley, 1990

Understanding Wine
Michael Schuster
Mitchell Beazley, 1989

How to Buy Fine Wine
Steven Spurrier
Phaidon Press, 1986

Academie du Vin Wine Course
Steven Spurrier
Mitchell Beazley

Sotheby's World Wine Encyclopaedia
Tom Stevenson
Sotheby, 1987

Dictionary of Wines and Spirits
Pamela Vandyke-Price
Northwood, 1980

The Mitchell Beazley Pocket Guide to
Fortified and Dessert Wines
Roger Voss
Mitchell Beazley, 1987

The Pocket Book on Cabernet Sauvignon
Wines
Roger Voss
Mitchell Beazley, 1988

The Pocket Book on Chardonnay Wine
Roger Voss
Mitchell Beazley, 1988

DESSERT WINES

Book of Dessert Wines
Mitchell Beazley, 1987

AUSTRALIA

Complete Book of Australian Wine
Len Evans
Facts-on-File, 1991

Pocket Guide to Australian & New
Zealand Wines
Jane MacQuitty
Mitchell Beazley, 1989

CHILE

Chilean Wines
Jan Read
Sotheby, 1985

FRANCE
French White Wines &
French Red and Rosé Wines (2 vols)
Oz Clarke
Sainsbury, 1989
The Wines of France
Clive Coates MW
Random Century, 1990

Wine Atlas of France
Hugh Johnson
Mitchell Beazley, 1988

The White Wines of France
Robert Joseph
Salamander, 1990

Larousse Wines & Vineyards of France
Ebury Press, 1990

Alsace

The Wines of Alsace
Liz Berry
Bodley Head, 1984

Alsace Wines
Pamela Vandyke-Price with Christopher
Fielden
Sotheby, 1988

Bordeaux

The Wines of Bordeaux
Edmund Penning-Rowsell
Penguin, 1989

Bordeaux
David Peppercorn MW
Faber & Faber, 1991

Bordeaux
Robert Parker
Dorling Kindersley

Burgundy

White Burgundy
Christopher Fielden
Christopher Helm, 1986

The Wines of Chablis
Rosemary George MW
Sotheby, 1984

Burgundy
Anthony Hanson
Faber & Faber, 1982

Burgundy
Robert Parker
Dorling Kindersley

Loire

The Loire Valley and its Wines
James Seely
Lennard Publishing, 1985

Rhône

Guide to the Wines of the Rhône
Peter Hallgarten
Pitman, 1986

The Wines of the Rhône
J Livingstone-Learmouth & Melvyn Master
Faber & Faber, 1987

The Wines of the Rhône Valley & Provence
Robert Parker
Dorling Kindersley

GERMANY

The Atlas of German Wines
Hugh Johnson
Mitchell Beazley, 1986

Life Beyond Liebfraumilch - Understanding
German Wine
Stuart Pigott
Sidgwick & Jackson, 1988

ITALY

Italian Wines
Maureen Ashley MW
Sainsbury, 1990

Chianti and the Wines of Tuscany
Rosemary George MW
Sotheby 1990

The Wines of Italy
David Gleave, Salamander 1989

NEW ZEALAND

The Wines and Vineyards of New
Zealand
Michael Cooper
Hodder & Stoughton 1988

Pocket Guide to Australian and New
Zealand Wines
Jane MacQuitty
Mitchell Beazley 1989

SOUTH AFRICA

The Complete Book of South African Wine
John Kench, Phyllis Hands, David Hughes
C Struick, Cape Town 1982

SPAIN & PORTUGAL

The Wines of Portugal
Jan Read
Faber & Faber 1987

The Wines of Spain and Portugal
Charles Metcalfe and Kathryn McWhirter
Salamander

USA

Pictorial Atlas of North American Wines
Thomas K Hardy
Grape Vision Pty Ltd 1990

The Pocket Encyclopaedia of California
Wines
Bob Thompson
Simon & Schuster 1989

Books for Cooks, 4 Blenheim Crescent,
London W11 Tel: 071 221 1992
food and wine book specialists, will mail
any of the books listed.

GLOSSARY

Acid/Acidity A wine with too much acidity and, therefore, unpleasantly sharp. Not well balanced.

Acidity Essential ingredient and preservative in all wines, which gives 'zest' to white wines, 'grip' to red wines and contributes to a good balance.

Appellation Contrôlée The French term which guarantees by law the geographic origins of a wine and the methods of vinification, though not necessarily its quality. All such wines declare this designation on the label, often abbreviated as AC or AOC. Many countries have similar designations.

Balance The harmonious blend of the major constituents in wine. Fruit, acidity, tannin and alcohol.

Blending Making wine from one or more grapes to produce the required taste. The blends for Quality wines must come from within a specified region.

Body A trade term for the weight of a wine. A combination of alcohol, fruit and acids.

Botrytis Cinerea See 'noble rot'.

Chaptalisation Increasing the strength, not sweetness of wine by adding sugar for conversion into alcohol.

Château More often an estate or farm than a castle. The Château may have several different vineyard plots, but all will take the name of the property, e.g. Ch Lafite will bottle the wines from all its vineyards under the single name of the château.

Claret The traditional British word for red Bordeaux wines. The word is not allowed by EC law to be used except in the UK!

Classic Grapes These are the grapes that produce the world's finest wines and are grown and distributed around the world.

Cloying Denotes a sweet wine lacking in acidity and therefore unbalanced.

Commune French for a parish. A commune wine will come from anywhere within the parish boundary.

Côte French for hillside and often used to denote vineyards spread along a hilly range.

Côte d'Or The golden slopes of Burgundy where the best vineyards are sited. Comprising the Côte de Beaune and Côte de Nuits, stretching from Dijon to Santenay.

Cru (Cru Classé, Premier Cru, Grand Cru,) Literally, the French for 'growth'. In wine terms it refers to a single vineyard, e.g. Ch Leoville Barton, 2ème Cru, in Bordeaux or Chablis Fourchaume, Premier Cru, in Burgundy. Cru Classé is a term reserved for the top flight Bordeaux wines. The terms Premier and Grand Cru are used elsewhere in France.

Cru Bourgeois A Bordeaux classification for second divison vineyards, i.e. those which rank below the Crus Classés.

Degrees The degrees of alcohol contained in the wine. Expressed as a percentage of alcohol by volume, e.g. 10.5%

Domaine In French means 'estate'.

Fermentation The primary process by which grape juice is turned into wine, by the action of yeast working on the grape sugar.

Flabby A trade term used to describe a wine lacking in acidity.

Generic Wine Describes wines by type or region, rather than by grape, e.g. fortified wine, sparkling wine, Chablis, Bordeaux.

Late Harvest Term used in the 'New World' to describe wines made from late-picked grapes, therefore producing more sweetness and concentration of fruit. As the wines get sweeter, terms – in ascending order of sweetness – such as Special, Select, or Special Select, will be added.

Macération Carbonique Fermentation of uncrushed grapes in sealed tanks.

Micro-Climate The climate of a small area which differs for any number of reasons from the general climate of the whole region.

Moelleux Literal translation is mellow, but in wine terms means sweet.

Must Crushed grapes or grape juice prior to fermentation.

Noble Late Harvest Term used in the 'New World' to denote late-picked grapes affected by 'botrytis' (see 'noble rot').

Noble Rot A benign fungus called 'botrytis cinerea' which rots and shrivels the grapes to produce superb sweet white wines.

Oak-Aged The process of maturing wines in oak casks before bottling, to give complexity of taste. Adds tannin.

Quality Wine In the legal sense, EC wines from specified regions made from specified grapes. However, we import wines of quality from many other countries which, by EC law, may only be called 'wine'.

Sec French word for dry.

Superieur Generic, regional wines, e.g. Beaujolais Superieur. Sounds grand but merely denotes that the wine has a little more alcohol than plain Beaujolais.

Süssreserve The addition of unfermented grape juice before bottling, to increase sweetness.

Tannin Bitter tasting element in red wines which comes from the grape skins, stalks, pips and oak-ageing. Acts as a preservative. Harshness reduces with age.

Tartrate Crystals Small crystals arising from the important tartaric acid present in all wines and usually removed before bottling. Although unsightly, the crystals fall rapidly to the bottom of the bottle or glass. They are harmless and do not affect the taste.

Vineyard An area where vines are planted and from which wines take their name. This can refer to a large area, e.g. Burgundy, France, or Napa Valley, California, comprising all its vineyards. More usually, it refers to a single vineyard or property, e.g. Meursault Les Charmes or Ch Latour, Bordeaux.

Vintage Denotes the year of the harvest, i.e. in which all the grapes have been picked, crushed and turned into wine.

Volume The amount of wine in the bottle.

Weight See under 'Body'.

INDEX

ORDER FORM
(you may photocopy this page if you wish)

MASKING LABELS

The ingenious way to entertain friends,
remove prejudice and discover your taste.
Each label is numbered and reusable, with
self-adhesive velcro.

Per pack of 4
£4.00 plus 50p p&p (UK only)

THE WINE TRACKER

Unravel the mystery of the wine shelves. The Wine
Tracker helps you select the style of wine you enjoy.
This revolutionary product helps you to find – by grape,
country and region – other wines you may also enjoy.
White wines are on one side, reds on the reverse.

Special price for readers of
How To Win The Wine Game
£6.00 plus 50p p&p (UK only)

PLAYING THE GAME – 2-BOTTLE & 12-BOTTLE TASTING AND GIFT CASES

Peter Noble has chosen for you a range of wines for PLAYING THE GAME and a series of gift cases

- ✂ -

To: The Grape Connection Ltd, PO Box 18, Hedge End, Southampton, Hants SO3 4QT

Please send me: ☐   pack(s) of 4 masking labels @ £4.50 per pack   ....

☐   Wine Tracker(s)   @ £6.50 each   ....

TOTAL : £ _____

☐   details of tasting and gift cases – please tick box

Cheques should be made payable to THE GRAPE CONNECTION LTD
or debit VISA/ACCESS account (delete where applicable).
Orders can be accepted over the telephone on 081 940 7576

Card No. ☐☐☐☐ ☐☐☐☐ ☐☐☐☐ ☐☐☐☐   Expiry Date _____

Name _____

Address _____

_____

Telephone No. _____   Signature _____   Date _____